CW00500535

Choirs and Cloisters

Seventy years of music in
church, college, cathedral
and Chapels Royal

by

Frederic Hodgson

Foreword by James Bowman

*To Pauline Snow
With all good wishes
from
Frederic Hodgson*

Thames Publishing

London

To the memory of my beloved wife, Beth, in deepest gratitude, and with love to my sons, John and Chris, and all the members of my family

Second edition
© 1995 Frederic Hodgson

CONTENTS

Illustrations between pages 72–73.

ACKNOWLEDGEMENTS

My gratitude and thanks are due to the celebrated countertenor, James Bowman, for his excellent foreword and support; and I am indebted to Dr Percy M Young, and to my son, Dr John T Hodgson, for their invaluable assistance.

My special thanks are also due to the following for photographs:

Mrs O Riggall	(Dr G J Bennett)
Mrs M Brockway	(Sir William Harris)
Tom Pinder	(Sir William Harris – presentation)
Neville Wridgway	(Dr Sidney Campbell and choristers)
Ronald H Smith	(Malcolm Boyle and Sir John Barbirolli)
Brian Pratt	('Chuck' – the Cloisters cat)
Alfred Hepworth	(Frederic Hodgson as a Gentleman of the Chapel Royal)
	(Chapel Royal staff)
	(Quartet)
Raymond Harper	(Beth Hodgson)
Geoffrey Shaw	(Choirs of St Paul's Cathedral and the Chapel Royal)
Alan Kendall	(Horseshoe Cloisters, Windsor Castle)

I am also especially grateful to my son, Chris Hodgson, for his drawings of Sheffield Cathedral, St Michael's College, Tenbury, Lincoln Cathedral, St George's Chapel, Windsor Castle, and the Chapel Royal, St James's Palace. Many thanks also to my grandson, Mark Hodgson, for his meticulous preparation of the typescript.

FOREWORD TO THE SECOND EDITION

I have read this unique book several times since it first appeared in 1988; I never fail to be fascinated by the extraordinary wealth of detail contained in it.

Cathedral music, thankfully, continues to flourish, despite the inevitable financial constraints, but so little is actually known about the numerous singers and organists who kept such a tradition alive for so long, especially in the years before the Second World War.

This book is a testament above all to a now largely forgotten generation of singers, many of whom seemed to come from Yorkshire. They all willingly gave the best years of their singing lives to our cathedral choirs; their loyalty and dedication to their chosen profession was truly remarkable. In the 1930s, lay-clerks could exist on their cathedral salaries and were able to enjoy a degree of job security unheard of nowadays, but they enjoyed none of the extra rewards that come from the wider world of recordings and television, to say nothing of opera; these benefits all came much later, in the 1960s. Thus, there are sadly few surviving recordings of these legendary singers.

Freddy Hodgson is one of the last members of this vanished generation, and he is justly proud to have been associated with them. Without this painstaking labour of love, many distinguished and faithful servants of our cathedral tradition would be forgotten.

James Bowman
August 1995

INTRODUCTION

After an exceptionally long and varied career in 'Quires and Places where they sing', these memoirs are the result of a general request from many church musicians. But they are also intended for others who might appreciate a few intimate glimpses into that august and somewhat esoteric world centred around the music of the church, which through the possession of a singing skill I have endeavoured to grace as a professional singer in churches, cathedrals, colleges, and famous royal foundations such as St George's Chapel, Windsor Castle, and HM Chapels Royal, St James's Palace. It has been my privilege to have taken part in many royal and state occasions, including the Coronation of HM Queen Elizabeth the Second in Westminster Abbey in 1953, and also at her Jubilee Thanksgiving Service in St Paul's Cathedral in 1977.

'Don't you get bored with singing so many services, day after day?' I have been asked. I have known those who have been bored, but my answer is an emphatic 'no', for in what better aesthetic environment could one wish to work than in our incomparable cathedrals and collegiate churches? One would have to be insensitive indeed not to be influenced by the architecture, or fail to gain inspiration from being part of the glorious heritage of church music which dedicated musicians in all ages have striven to preserve, and which has enhanced worship through the centuries.

Members of professional choirs are sometimes accused of being merely performers, or 'musical instruments', who are apt to regard services more as concerts than acts of worship. Nothing is further from the truth with the genuinely dedicated choral singer, who could never be regarded as mercenary, as the financial rewards are slender. But with fewer services to contend with since the Second World War, cathedral singers of today, many of whom have been choral scholars in universities, enjoy a far greater freedom to augment their stipends from outside sources, often as teachers. Their predecessors, who in most cases were committed to attending two services every day at inconvenient times, had to supplement their stipends as best they could. Broadcasting, television, recordings, recitals and foreign tours now provide greater opportunities for choral singers than ever before.

As I retrace my steps through a maze of spires, domes, towers and cloisters, I shall hope to take the reader with me on a pilgrimage extending well over half a century, where it will be seen that running through the rich tapestry of dignity, solemnity, fanfares and pageantry is a thread of humour which convinces me that God loves fun.

I have always had an eye for the Church's lighter side, and a sense of humour is a desideratum if one is to debunk the pomposity, and overcome that frustration and bitterness not unknown to many who spend their lives in the service of the Church. It is well known that since long before the time of Trollope, relationships in cathedral communities, and particularly between next-door neighbours, have often been far from happy, and contrary to what one would expect among professing Christians living together in the beauty of such environments. Many years ago I asked a priest vicar at one cathedral why he had stayed 50 years in the same post, and had never sought preferment. He was a scholar and an excellent musician. 'My boy,' he replied, 'I have been perfectly content. When I first came here, I learned to laugh, and I have laughed ever since. Go and do thou likewise.' I could well believe him, as I never saw a more jovial face. In an age when the Church of England is in a sad decline, and the world seems to have stopped laughing, would that there were more with his philosophy.

The terms lay clerk, lay vicar, vicar choral, and songman all designate the cathedral singing man.

CHAPTER ONE
A Yorkshire musical apprenticeship

As a native Yorkshireman – born in Sheffield – I had one natural advantage: choral singing was in the blood. The dominating figure in the district was the great Sir Henry Coward, who began life as apprentice in a Sheffield cutlery works. He applied himself with such diligence that he eventually became a Doctor of Music of Oxford University, and by his inspiration brought the Sheffield Choir to international fame. Elgar once described the choir as 'absolutely the finest in the world'.

There was a plethora of enthusiastic choral and operatic societies, male-voice choirs and quartets, and church and chapel choirs. Music and singing teachers with brass plates on their doors abounded, and LRAMs, ARCMs, LTCLs, ALCMs, etc, all vied with each other. A decorative appendage to one's name was something to be envied. Bogus organisations were quick to exploit the situation, and spurious qualifications proliferated.

Such a condition could not fail to inspire the characteristic Yorkshire humour, as in the case of the brass-band player who lived in a street where musical qualifications were displayed on every door except his own. Not to be outdone, he placed a huge board outside his house, which read: BILL SYKES, B.B.B.B.B.B. When his puzzled neighbours asked what the letters meant, he answered proudly: 'BEST BLOODY BASS IN T'BRIGHTSIDE BRASS BAND'.

There was an amusing competitive element (exasperating to choirmasters) among some amateur choralists who evidently preferred to be judged on the quantity of the tone they could produce, rather than on the quality, and to whom such inhibitions as blend and balance were anathema. Which recalls the old Corney Grain song of the boy chorister, 'Whose voice o'ertopped the rest, which was very inartistic, but the public liked it best.' It was not unusual to hear some proud relative declare: 'Our Joe's best singer in t'choir; you can hear him sing above all t'others.'

In those days singing provided a ready escape from the grime of the cutlers' shops, the forges, the 'dark Satanic mills', the stuffy offices and slavish shops. But the ever-present pall of smoke thinned out at the city's periphery, through which one could pass into the pure air of the glorious heather-clad moors, dales, hills and woods of the Peak District of Derbyshire.

'The ugly picture in a beautiful frame' came to be a popular description of Sheffield. But in recent years smokeless zoning has done much to clean the air. Whenever I visit Sheffield now I am always taken on a pilgrimage through the city centre by a brother-in-law, John Russell, who is as loyal and as typical a Sheffielder as could be found. With great pride, he never fails in a ritual of inviting me to breathe in deeply of the fresh air, which I find incredible after the fug of my youth.

Sheffielders have always been ready to defend their city of iron and steel and its environs against all criticism, and this has developed into an almost fanatical chauvinism and insularity, particularly when extolling the virtues of the nearby incomparable Derbyshire, while still remaining 'reight good Yorkshire'.

Football has been a dominant and integral part of the Sheffield scene for over a century, and there is good reason to believe that it was here that the game as it is known throughout the world today had its birth. There has always been a fierce partisanship between the supporters of Sheffield United and Sheffield Wednesday. I have often heard it said that no true Wednesdayite (colours blue and white) would conscientiously eat bacon, as its colours are those of United (red and white). What is there about football which so exclusively captivates spectators? Is it that the grizzled old man recaptures his youth? Or does the cripple 'run' with the fastest player? Do the masses of fans have their moment of personal triumph and achievement as each one of them enters that glorious realm of fantasy to become one with their idol as he scores that magnificent goal? If this game weaves such magic spells, then it justifies its existence, in spite of the tarnishing of its image by the rampant hooliganism of recent years. It is to be hoped that sanity can be soon restored to the terraces. The game is thus summed up by Edward Carpenter, former Dean of Westminster, who is probably football's most ardent clerical fan: 'Football is a religious exercise, a ritual of high expertise. Watching is an exhausting occupation, and they ought to let old men play, while the young engage in the ritual on the terraces, and do not despise soccer when thinking of the world's moral progress.'

* * *

My singing career virtually began in infancy, and my doting parents never missed an opportunity of recounting how I could sing nursery rhymes 'perfectly in tune' before I was three years old. Such precocity may arouse scepticism, but a life-long sense of perfect pitch tends to corroborate that claim. As a boy I would wander around Sheffield streets identifying the pitch of sounds such as motor-horns, tramcar bells, the cries of street vendors and stallholders in the market, and checking them triumphantly with a pitchpipe or tuning-fork.

The characteristic variations of the Yorkshire dialect as spoken in Sheffield have evolved into a kind of 'Sheffieldese' or 'Sheffieldish', and many a stranger has needed an interpreter. Some years ago, at the College of Education, students from other parts of the country sent out on teaching practice found it necessary to be equipped with a glossary of terms and phrases in general use among schoolchildren to understand what was said. One glance at these brought back my boyhood, and particularly my choirboy days. Talking during services might bring an admonishment from a senior boy with a fiercely whispered 'shut thi gob'. A misunderstanding or inattentiveness or even singing out of tune met with 'tha wants to wesh thi earoils out'. Someone might bring a message: 'we've gorra gerrus imbux'. A boy who was fooling around was ordered to stop 'manking about', and anyone who was deliberately absent from practice or service was accused of 'duffing it' or playing t'wag. Some words had been coined, such as 'hangment', presumably a euphemism for the word hell, and a corruption of 'hamlet', used in the context of 'playing hell' ('he was in such a temper that he played hangment'). These are but a few examples of the colourful jargon peculiar to Sheffield. The relationship between such speech characteristics, and particular love of and skill in singing, calls for closer examination, I feel.

In a city renowned for its fine singing voices and musicians, for which, of course, a sensitive ear is imperative, it has always seemed paradoxical to me that over the generations so little aesthetic impact has been made on the flat monotonous timbre of the speaking voices of so many natives of Sheffield. This local sound cannot be associated entirely with the regular use of dialect and the broad vowels of the working classes, as it can be detected from time to time in otherwise 'well-spoken' professional classes, which suggests that it is something indigenous to Sheffielders, evolving perhaps from aural imitation. I have always been able to identify this ubiquitous Sheffield voice wherever I have travelled at home and abroad, and as Sheffielders, with their spontaneous warmth and wit as sharp as their world-famed cutlery, are the salt of the earth, that salt has its own particular savour.

I joined my first church choir before I was six years of age, and I well remember my excitement as I trotted hand-in-hand with my father down a Sheffield street to St Simon's Church (long since demolished). This was not quite unfamiliar to me, for my father – a dental surgeon by profession – sang tenor in the choir. I was so tiny that when I appeared in the vestry, someone said: 'He's nobbut a babby!' The smallest cassock was too large, and it tripped me up as I ascended the chancel steps. My father said this was a good omen.

I later became a member of several city choirs, including the Cathedral, and I also became well known as a soloist in churches, chapels, concert halls and cinemas. I am told that I had the traditional cherubic face of the choirboy, which by rigid discipline I learned early in life to keep straight and innocent-looking at least. As is well known, laughter and the giggles are always hard to suppress in church. This facial control developed in me a *sang froid* which enabled me to sail through many an awkward confrontation familiar to any chorister following some prank or other. As one who has taught thousands of schoolchildren to sing, I have seen that self-same look, betrayed only by the telltale twinkle in the eye, on many a young face, and by spanning the years (as one little horror to another) I have understood!

One of the pranks which stands out in my memory was the enforced initiation of new choirboys at St Augustine's Church. When the coast was clear the lad was 'led' into the darkened nave, where rays from the street lamps filtered eerily through the windows. The boy was placed in a pew and told to look upwards. Other boys, hidden from view, some up in the pulpit, would be waiting with their surplices screwed up into a ball. At a given signal they would fling these high into the air, and as they floated down they would open out like so many flapping ghosts, to the accompaniment of spine-chilling wails.

At St Mary's Church, Walkley, a small honorarium was paid to choirboys once a quarter, and was eagerly awaited. Senior boys received five shillings, and the newest recruit was given sixpence. One very young newcomer was told very solemnly that his first pay would be so large that he would need a wheelbarrow to carry it home. He took this literally, and turned up on 'pay-neet' actually trundling a small barrow. The choirmaster saw the joke, and the sixpence was deposited ceremoniously into the barrow, with the boy joining in the fun, being wheeled home, triumphantly clutching his first pay.

It was customary for choirboys to wear Eton collars and mortarboards as standard uniform. Rubber collars were allowed, and were favoured as they only needed to be wiped clean; but they soon turned yellow. The more fastidious, however, sported starched linen collars, and mine went to the local Chinese laundry, which in those days had a kind of oriental mystique, heightened by the approach of shuffling feet and the appearance through a sliding panel of a bland, inscrutable face and a glimpse of a pigtail. A ticket with Chinese characters was handed through the panel, followed by a high-pitched comment: 'Collee done Slaturday, thank you much.' Then the panel was slammed to. It was said that the laundering was done by a secret process (which hazarded some preposterous guesses!) But whatever it was produced the finest starched collar I have ever seen.

Walkley Church maintained a musical tradition for many years, and settings to the canticles and anthems covering an extensive repertoire were sung regularly. And how those boys could sing! The church has been fortunate in being able to boast such gifted organists as Cyril Cantrell (father of Derek Cantrell, the Manchester Cathedral organist), and Dr George Linstead, distinguished critic and scholar, of Sheffield University, and one of the best-known musicians in the north. My own dear father derived great joy from singing in that choir. An abiding memory is of him processing down the nave and singing with such gusto until he nearly lost his balance!

His devoted Aberdeen terrier, 'Nigger', had an uncanny sense of service times. He would slip unnoticed through the west door as the choir processed, and walk with my father up the aisle, with head cocked to attract his attention, which convulsed choir and congregation.

Often during a service the muffled rattle of a tin of 'Meloids' in the hands of a corner-boy would turn every head in his direction, followed by a whispered command: 'Give us one – pass'em up.'

After some furtive fumbling the small black throat pellets, including those which had spilled on the floor, were passed up the line of boys from hand to hand, all hot, sticky and fluffy.

A hilarious occasion was provided by a visiting preacher, who in a paroxysm of coughing parted with his dentures. These landed at the foot of a sidesman, who picked them up deftly with his handkerchief and handed them back. With a few toothless sibilants the embarrassed parson brought his sermon to a premature close.

At a harvest festival, as a corner-boy I was standing tantalisingly near to a huge bunch of grapes hanging from the end of the stall. The anthem leading me towards temptation was *O taste and see*, by Goss.

The curate at Walkley in those days was the Rev E H P Rawlins. He came from Birmingham and had red hair, and if ever a young parson had fire in his belly, he had. His preaching was so dramatic that he could even hold the attention of the choirboys (though it may have been that he was apt to lean dangerously out of the pulpit). This was no mean feat. The modern choirboy sometimes brings a book – or a comic – to pass the sermon time. That there has been a decline in preaching cannot be denied, and preachers who were convincing orators seem to belong to the past. A well-known canon was heard to say recently: 'Well! Who wants sermons anyway?' This sentiment is apparently shared by many trendy clap-happy clergy with their trite hymns, more of politicians than priests, whose ideologies, derived from the pop scene and gimmicks such as adopting the style and vocabulary of the latest trendsetter as aids to worship 'relevant to modern society', have offended the faithful rather than filled the empty pews with young folk: they have certainly driven many an organist away.

Rawlins later became a Canon and Precentor of Sheffield Cathedral. He always kept in touch with his old boys, and we remained lifelong friends. As a whitehaired octogenarian, some of the fire may have gone out of him, but he could still put over a fine sermon. Whenever we met he always greeted me with outstretched hands, and the clock turned back to those far-off days at Walkley Church. I could see standing before me the red-headed firebrand thundering from the pulpit, or my scoutmaster in shorts and red hairy knees. No doubt he recalled me as a small boy in cassock and surplice and beautifully starched Eton collar, or as a boy-scout with smooth, bare knees.

My lengthy association with clergy has been mainly with Dean and Chapter, the ecclesiastical elite of the cathedral close. Many of these dignitaries would seem throughout the ages to have maintained a dictatorial or negative and indifferent attitude to church music and its musicians, an attitude which is as notorious as it is inexplicable. One of the reasons may be that so many of the clergy are unmusical, and therefore likely to regard music as nothing more than a mere adjunct to worship, and to consider that too much importance is placed on it. Dean Inge (the 'gloomy Dean') of St Paul's was tone deaf, and used to complain about having to endure so many musical services; he would show his resentment by reading a book while the singing went on. Sometimes he wondered 'whether people thought the Deity enjoyed being serenaded'. But can such unappreciative people really be oblivious to the fact that countless souls have been inspired by, and have gained their greatest spiritual comfort through, music beautifully rendered in church?

Here we would do well to recall the famous Samuel Sebastian Wesley, whose centenary was celebrated in 1976. Successively organist of Hereford and Exeter Cathedrals, Leeds Parish Church, and Winchester and Gloucester Cathedrals, he achieved more for the church than most of the ecclesiastical establishment who either derided or feared him. As is well known, he was constantly in conflict with clergy, and he went so far as to suggest that they should no longer be resident in their posts, but that a central headquarters should be established which would send out priests (presumably musical ones) to conduct services. A drastic and not very practical innovation, I am sure! It is on record that his personal comment after an exceptionally long sermon was to play the Dead March in *Saul*.

There have, of course, always been the notable exceptions among Deans and Chapters, and indeed other clergy who have appreciated their organists and choirs, and have been much concerned about their welfare. I am told that the late Dr A V Baillie, when he was Dean of Windsor, was a particular friend to the lay clerks of St George's Chapel, and augmented their stipends out of his own pocket. He said that at one time the lay clerks were his only friends.

I continued to sing treble until I was 18 years of age, which was considered exceptional. But my voice never actually 'broke' at the normal changing period. The transition from treble to alto was immediate, without any cessation in singing. It may be of interest to quote a passage from 'The Contemporary Alto', an article I wrote for the *Musical Times* (April 1965, p 293), which refers to the unbroken voice:

> The high-pitched tenor or countertenor can be described as a natural voice, but the controversial question as to whether there can be an unbroken natural alto voice crops up from time to time. There is no doubt that such a voice exists, but it is a physiological aberration. It can only occur where, during puberty (while physical development in every other respect is progressing normally), there is scarcely any lengthening of the vocal cords, or appreciable growth in the associated ligaments and muscles, thus leaving the voice virtually unbroken. In such a case the youth usually continues to sing treble until he is well in his teens, with only a gradual loss of the extreme upper register, and at its best, the voice matures at manhood into a pure full tone. There is no break, the voice being homogeneous throughout a wide compass (some tenors claim to have unbroken voices).

Before leaving Sheffield I sang alto at the cathedral, which used to be known affectionately as 't'owd church', and at J L Pearson's lovely church of St John, Ranmoor. The choirmen at Sheffield Cathedral are known as Songmen (as they are at York Minster), and I recall my feelings of awe for my older colleagues, who were very conscious of their position. I was soon given to understand that it was 'summat to be in t'cathedral choir'. Many of them had really excellent robust Yorkshire voices; they had a tremendous enthusiasm for their singing, and there was a high standard of performance.

At that time Sheffield was justifiably proud of its tramcars, which for comfort and reliability and general efficiency could well have been an object lesson for our present-day transport failings. The trams disappeared in 1960 (and made a welcome reappearance in 1994). On Sunday mornings the Songmen could be seen alighting from trams near the cathedral. How they looked the part, with their bowler hats, wing collars, spats and umbrellas! They strutted across the cathedral yard with a determined look which suggested that they could master whatever was placed before them. With the assistance of the organist, T W Hanforth, they invariably did. They were kind and encouraging to me, and the time I spent with them was valuable experience.[1]

---

[1] During the last war, while on war service, I was posted to Sheffield. I rejoined the Cathedral choir, and sang there for two-and-a-half years. The great welcome I received from the organist, Dr R Tustin Baker, and the Songmen, after such a long absence, could never be forgotten.

I was also a member of an enthusiastic male-voice quartet. My three colleagues, Alwyne Banks, Reginald Crookes and Edwin Hague, were all fine and well-known local singers. The venue of our rehearsals must have been unique, for often late in the evening we would gather round the dental chair in my father's surgery, which overlooked a busy main road. On one occasion the final cadence of a part-song had scarcely died away when there were loud cheers from outside. Somewhat embarrassed, I went to the door and peered out. Standing on the pavement was an audience of youths. 'Oh, it's thee and thi pals, Freddy, is it', said one of them. 'We thowt it was thi fatther pulling somebody's 'eead off!'

One Sunday afternoon we were giving a recital in a large methodist chapel, and the organist gave us the wrong chord to start *God is a Spirit*, by Sterndale Bennett — another Sheffield man. We were waiting for the chord of B flat and he gave us E flat. We knew at once, and it would have been disastrous (not to say dangerous) to have attempted to sing it in a higher key. There was an awkward pause, and then Ted Hague, the bass, looking up at the organ, called out, 'B flat please'. Then in a real stage whisper which nearly ruined everything, he hissed, 'He thinks we're eunuchs!' It was that first quartet which fostered in me a lifelong love of male-voice singing, and in later years, as a member of several professional quartets, I have often recalled those early experiences with — one may aptly say — glee.

It had been assumed that I should follow the family profession of dentistry. But a preliminary visit to Sheffield University with my father, where I was led innocently into a dissection room, was a traumatic experience which put an end to all that.

CHAPTER TWO
St Michael's College, Tenbury

At the age of 19 I left Sheffield to take up my first professional appointment, as a lay clerk at St Michael's College, Tenbury. Set remote in the beautiful Worcestershire countryside, two miles from the nearest small market town of Tenbury Wells, this famous choral foundation came into being through the inspiration of Sir Frederick Arthur Gore Ouseley, one of the more significant of Victorian church musicians. A clergyman brought up in an environment which caused him to come to maturity with a great concern for the liturgy of the Church of England, as established in the Prayer Book, and its music, he built St Michael's mostly at his own expense. It was inaugurated splendidly in 1856, and the solo treble at the consecration was Arthur Sullivan, borrowed for the occasion from the Chapel Royal, St James's. It was fortunate, perhaps, that the Master of the Children of the Chapel Royal was Thomas Helmore, a Worcestershire man. The organist for the occasion was John Stainer, who accepted a permanent appointment but stayed only for two years at Tenbury before proceeding to distinguished appointments at Oxford and in London.

Ouseley was much influenced by the driving power of the Oxford Movement at a time when the Church of England generally, and church music in particular, were in a deplorable state. He intended his new college to provide a model choir whose influence would be widespread, which in due course it was. Many old boys, organists and singers, have risen to positions of eminence, both clerical and lay, in the Church.

An excellent example of the earlier Gothic revival, it was the first collegiate church to be founded in England since the Reformation. Its music library was acknowledged throughout the world as an important source library. Its most prized possession was the score of *Messiah* from which Handel conducted the first performance, in Dublin in 1742.

I took up my appointment at Michaelmas, and had lodgings at The Brackens, a red-brick house set picturesquely in the gorse and bracken of Old Wood Common. The kindly and motherly ministrations of my landlady, Mrs Mapp (formerly well known to generations of undergraduates at Oxford), helped to dispel the initial nostalgia for home and parents. But I was soon under the spell of that delectable countryside, of which H C Colles once said:

> Its pastures, its springing crops, with wild roses in the hedgerows, its orchards when the fruit is firmly set; its prospects, Clee Hill across the Common to the north, the woods and uplands of Worcestershire to the south; all call the traveller to stay. (*History of St Michael's College, Tenbury*, ed M F Alderson and H C Colles, London 1943).

On the founding of the Friends of St Michael's College in 1981, Sir John Betjeman wrote:

> I like to think of that independent kingdom where St Michael's College stands and of Henry Woodyer's marvellous gothic which I shall always remember.
>
> I am very glad you are founding 'Friends of St Michael's', it needs friends for it is unique and Anglican; all the country round it sings. I love the place.

There were the inevitable characters, some of whom have become legendary. Barrie Maund, a fine deep bass had been in the choir for 40 years, and his loyalty and attachment to St Michael's was such that he had resisted many offers of more lucrative appointments elsewhere. He was tall, with a tremendous belly, and as he processed into the choirstalls it was fascinating to see him hoist this great pendulous mass and flop it on to his stall.

Arthur Perry Cox, the tenor and general factotum of the College for 44 years, could do anything in the way of repairs as well as he could sing. 'I sing for my Maker', he would say, which in these material and godless days says much for men who were so dedicated that they were content to spend their lives in such a remote and isolated place on stipends which were a ridiculous pittance.

Claude Norris, an excellent bass, later became a celebrated lay vicar of Salisbury Cathedral. He and Horace Rose, my alto colleague, and I all lodged together at The Brackens, and were firm friends.

Horace John Earl Rose was a middle-aged bachelor with a beautiful fluty alto voice. A former schoolmaster, he was cultured, kindly, but very eccentric. Claude and I nicknamed him 'Noble', by which he was known for years. He was a semi-invalid as a result of the war of 1914—1918 and after singing in several cathedral and London church choirs had opted for the rural scene on account of his health. The poor chap had developed a nervous phobia over the malfunctioning of his 'waterworks'. He would suddenly cease talking in the middle of a sentence when he received a 'call', and place his finger on his lips to motion silence, and steal from the room purposefully.

'Noble', and I must have made an odd-looking pair as we tramped the country lanes. He had a shambling gait, and wore an ancient, bashed-in trilby hat, and boots with the tags sticking up, while I loped alongside in plus-fours and rakish trilby hat with a curved brim. I wore this type of hat for many years (indeed I still do an occasion, even in these hatless days), and it became well known as 'Freddy's classical curve'. We would often sing alto as we walked, which must have scared many a rabbit back into its burrow. Farm labourers occasionally stopped in their tracks, and once a ruddy rustic peered nervously over a hedge, muttering, 'It's they durned singers from the college'.

One afternoon, as we swung along with *O thou that tellest* in full song, 'Noble' got an urgent call, and the mellifluous flow of his Handelian runs ceased abruptly. He motioned silence with his finger and went rapidly through a gate into a field, only to reappear seconds later, panting and with glassy eyes, making for the gate at speed, which he slammed to just in time to halt the thundering gallop of a huge bull. When he recovered his breath he looked at me sadly and said: 'Just my luck, another interrupted cadence'. (He seemed least concerned that it could have been a final cadence!)

There were some excellent musicians among the choirboys. The head chorister at that time was Newell Wallbank, who presented a memorable picture in his red cassock, white surplice and ruff, as he stood in the corridor adjoining the cloisters, saying the Prayer of Dismissal in beautifully modulated tones: 'Pardon, O Lord, all that Thou hast seen amiss in our service, and teach us to worship Thee more worthily'. Newell was in due course Organ Scholar at Queen's College, Cambridge, and after leaving Cambridge distinguished himself by becoming the youngest Doctor of Music of Trinity College, Dublin. He was ordained, and his career in the Church brought him in the fullness of time to the Rectory of St Bartholomew the Great, Smithfield, where music of all kinds is cultivated. He also became a Prebendary of St Paul's.

I was fortunate enough to spend two commemorations at St Michael's, which were always held on the Patronal Day at Michaelmas.

'Commem' was usually attended by many of the most distinguished clergy and church musicians of the day, and apart from the music I suppose the excellent food was an attraction. On one of these occasions, owing to the absence of 'Noble' through illness, I found myself the only alto, left to cope with a heavy bill of festival music. But there was no lack of gallant volunteers to come to the aid of such a lone young alto, and my new colleagues were none other than Sir Ivor Atkins, Organist of Worcester Cathedral and a close friend of Elgar, Dr Henry C Colles, celebrated music critic of *The Times*, and the Rev Dr Edmund H Fellowes, of St George's Chapel, Windsor, and the eminent music scholar and editor of much Tudor church music, of madrigals and lute songs (I was later to become associated with him at Windsor).[1] These distinguished gentlemen all insisted on singing with me on the Decani side, rather than distribute their talents antiphonally. As I listened incredulously, if somewhat ungratefully, to their combined efforts, I soon discovered that alto singing could not be included in their otherwise outstanding musical attainments.

Curiously enough, Dr Colles was prejudiced against the alto voice, as can be seen in his writings. His own efforts therefore may have been masochistic. Sir Ivor Atkins, with his white hair and moustache, was restricted by his exceptionally high stiff collar (known as a 'choker'), which obviously forced up his larynx to produce what he himself described as 'a bit of fruity alto'. As for Dr Fellowes, he did his best. But no commemoration was complete without excellent violin solos from him, while the boys always clamoured for his *tour-de-force* — a performance of Tallis's Canon accomplished by whistling and humming simultaneously. Another memory is of Sir Hugh Allen, Director of the Royal College of Music, sitting on the floor with the boys, absolutely fascinated by a model railway system.

After spending four memorable and happy terms at Tenbury, I decided the time had come for me to gain a cathedral appointment, and it was with great regret that I left the College and my many friends to take up an appointment as a lay vicar of Lincoln Cathedral. But St Michael's left an indelible mark on me, for the standard of music under the Warden, Rev E H Swann, formerly Precentor of Ripon, was very high. Towards the end of his wardenship — helped by his second wife, who had been a scholar at the Royal College of

---

[1] E H Fellowes was Librarian of St Michael's College for 30 years (1918 to 1948).

Music – Swann startled the neighbourhood by bringing together various friends to aid selected staff and pupils in performances of Purcell's *Dido and Aeneas* and Mozart's *The Magic Flute*.

An event unique in the history of St Michael's College occurred in October 1980, when George Coles completed 50 years as an outstanding bass lay clerk. An Evensong was held specially to celebrate the occasion, and tributes were paid to him by many distinguished musicians from all over the country, including the following from Sir David Willcocks: 'There can be few, if any, who have given such a wonderful service to the college since its foundation'. He was elected a Fellow of the College in 1968.

It is regrettable that I have to conclude this chapter on Tenbury on a sad note, for after maintaining the highest standards of church music for more than a century and a quarter in accordance with the Founder's wishes, the College had to close in 1985.

From the early 1980s there had been a steady decline in the number of pupils, which made the school 'no longer financially or educationally viable'. Desperate attempts were made to save the College, and an appeal was launched; but the necessary target could not be achieved, and there was no alternative but to bring to an end a glorious heritage. A closing Thanksgiving Service was held in July 1985. But no good influence is ever lost, and there could be no more appropriate words than those of Dr Runcie, Archbishop of Canterbury, who sent the following message:

My thoughts are with you as you prepare to hold your Service of Thanksgiving for the work and witness of St Michael's College over more than a century and a quarter.

With its magnificant library, the catalogue of distinguished musicians who have been members of its staff, and its illustrious list of Old Boys, St Michael's needs no help from me to secure its reputation. Thanks to the College, the standard of Cathedral music is higher today than it has ever been.

Though I shall be sharing your sadness that this happy and triumphant chapter in the history of the English Church and its music is drawing to a close, I shall also be thanking God for all that has been achieved since St Michael's was founded.

The College has completed its task, but the spirit of Tenbury will live on through all those who learned to love their Church and the music of St Michael's.

ROBERT CANTUAR

CHAPTER THREE

The cathedral tradition at Lincoln

'Beautiful for situation; the joy of the whole earth', 'How rise thy towers serene and bright'. The words of the Psalmist and of Samuel Johnson spring instinctively to one's lip when approaching Lincoln Cathedral, so majestic on its sovereign hill. John Ruskin said that it was 'worth two of any other English cathedrals', and William Cobbett described it as 'the finest building in the whole world'. Extravagant claims they may be, though fervently upheld by many ecclesiologists, artists and writers throughout the ages, and of all those countless multitudes who have been bewitched by its incomparable magnificence.

In one of his *Short Studies*, J A Froude has Lincoln in mind when he wrote: 'The Cathedral is the one object which possesses the imagination and refuses to be eclipsed'. He contrasts its exquisite beauty with the 'puny dwelling places of the citizens, which creep at its feet, and stream down the hill in motley confusion'.[1]

There can be no finer environment in which to sing than that of the Angel Choir, 'one of the loveliest of human works'. I was captivated by it when I first looked through the choir gates.

The famous Steep Hill up which one has to climb to reach the Cathedral (or Minster as it is commonly known) divides the city into 'uphill' and 'downhill', by which designations they are known locally. I first found lodgings 'uphill', where my landlady demonstrated a thrift which she had developed into a high expertise. Food was measured out microscopically, and she could perform miracles with a Sunday joint by serving it up in various guises throughout the week. There was a young maid-of-all-work who sympathised with my plight by slipping me many a surreptitious piece of cake or biscuit. The sitting room had but one easy chair, which I soon discovered was reserved exclusively for the landlady's dog, whose bared teeth and deep growl was as much a deterrent as the cynical grin on the face of its owner. In any case, the chair was covered in dog hairs! Such

[1] See T G Bonney, *Cathedrals, Abbeys and Churches*, London, 1898, p 78.

cold comfort drove me early to bed, which needed my overcoat to augment the one blanket. I soon escaped to more comfortable lodgings with my colleague, Tom Laidler.

I also discovered one had to be tough to withstand the biting winds which blow unimpeded over the flat country from the East Coast. 'So bracing', it has been called; others just describe it as expletive cold. But the warmth of the citizens was the great compensation, and I never met friendlier than those of Lincoln. I was invited to many houses, where I was only too pleased to sing for my supper. I had acquired a motorbike whilst I was at Tenbury, and as Lincoln was a little over 40 miles from Sheffield, I was able to pay weekly visits to my parents. What a joy it was on the return journey to watch those three towers of Lincoln grow from tiny dots on the horizon as I approached full throttle over the flat roads. But that motorbike (a Matchless) led me into all kinds of trouble, from skidding on ice through a hedge into a field, to turning over a barrow of apples in a market place, and to almost annihilating a cathedral organist, who stepped back just in time!

The organist when I arrived at Lincoln was Dr George John Bennett, who held the appointment for 35 years. Over the past two centuries length of service has characterised Lincoln, where organists have been described as a 'contented race'. In all that time there have been only seven: John Hasted (1784—94), George Skelton (1794—1850), John Young (1850—95), George John Bennett (1895—1930), Gordon Slater (1930—66), Philip Marshall (1966—86). This unbroken tradition of long-serving organists was brought to an end by the appointment of David Flood, who succeeded Philip Marshall in 1986, and left in 1988 in become organist of Canterbury Cathedral, where he had previously been assistant organist.[1]

William Byrd, possibly a native of Lincoln, was organist of the Cathedral from 1563 (when he was only 20) until appointments as Gentlemen and Organist of the Chapel Royal kept him in London. What Byrd wrote almost 400 years ago on introduction to his

---

[1] Hasted resigned the office without any reason being delivered to posterity. One suspects he was guilty of some impropriety, or was rude to the Dean — or both. Skelton, son of a local blacksmith, worked his way from being a chorister. Young, pupil of William Henshaw of Durham, did much to improve the standard of the cathedral music. He also left behind a specification for a new organ, which was used as a basis by Bennett and Henry Willis.

Psalms, Sonets and Songs is still relevant. The idea of a healthy mind and a healthy body was being vigorously promoted by Elizabethan educationists.

Here are Byrd's reasons − briefly set down by th'auctor − to persuade everyone to learn to sing:

1. First it is a knowledge easily taught, and quickly learned where there is a good Master and an apt Scoller.
2. The exercise of singing is delightfull to Nature and good to preserve the health of man.
3. It doth strengthen all parts of the brest, and doth open the pipes.
4. It is a singular good remedie for a stutting and stammering in the speech.
5. It is the best means to procure a perfect pronunciation and to make a good orator.
6. It is the onely way to know where Nature hath bestowed the benefit of a good voyce: which gift is so rare, as there is not one among a thousand, that hath it: and in many that excellent guift is lost, because they want Art to express Nature.
7. There is not any Musicke of Instruments whatsoever, comparable to that which is made of the voyces of Men, where the voyces are good, and the same well sorted and ordered.
8. The better the voyce is, the meeter it is to honour and to serve God therewith: and the voyce of man is chiefly to be employed to that ende.

omnis spiritus laudet Dominum.

Since singing is so good a thing
I wish all men would learne to sing.

It was certainly an experience to have sung under Dr Bennett. He was a chorister at Winchester College and a student at the Royal Academy of Music, where he later became Professor of Harmony. He studied the organ in Berlin and Munich under Kiel and Rheinberger. He was justly renowned for his extemporisations, his accompaniments − especially of the Psalms − and the singing, which he had raised to a superlatively high standard. He had that kind of unpredictable temperament which seems typical of many highly sensitive musicians; he could be as benign and charming as he could be irascible and hyper-critical. He was a large shambling figure with a white nicotine-stained moustache and a mane of hair. He wore a wide-brimmed Stetson type of hat which I envied.

One morning, in the crowded High Street, I spotted that unmistakeable hat, just as he had evidently caught sight of Freddy's 'classical curve'. He signalled me to cross the street, which meant a hazardous zig-zag through traffic. With the mystique of a conjurer he drew from his pocket a Byrd motet, and with huge finger he jabbed at a note in the alto part. 'Watch that carefully', he said, 'its a D natural'. He shambled off without another word.

At early morning practices a choirboy would stand at the top of the Song School steps keeping *cave* for the arrival of the Doctor. There would be the sound of laboured footsteps, but before he came into view, there would be a tremendous shout: 'Stanford in C', or whatever it was he wished to rehearse first. There was no excuse for not having the music ready. His huge hands wrought havoc to the long-suffering piano when he was not altogether pleased with the choir's efforts. I was never quite sure how true it was that a local music shop kept a man standing by to repair that piano. He was well-known for his habit of sticking his tobacco-stained fingers into a choirboy's mouth to get him to open it wide. But when, in a moment of aberration he meted out the same treatment to a lady he was auditioning for the Music Society, out shot her dentures!

Bennett kept a row of medicine bottles in the organ loft on a little ledge under the draw-stops on the left-hand side of the manuals, and many bottles of smelling salts. Clifford Hewis, assistant organist for many years until his retirement in 1975, tells the story of how at a service the Doctor cut his hand accidentally on a bottle without being aware of it, and Clifford had to mop up the blood from the keys of several manuals as he went on playing.

He had a peculiar habit of wagging his hand, which could be interpreted as an admonitory gesture or one of approval, according to mood. He would sometimes sit in the congregation during a service, while the assistant organist officiated, and I well remember the astonishment on people's faces when at Evensong one day he suddenly left his seat and walked down to the choirstalls, and took an erring boy by the ear and led him through the choirscreen. But he was always concerned about his boys. They were fond of him, and he helped them in many ways. He was generous and hospitable, and a visit to his home, North Place, usually ended in a game of billiards.

The four senior boys at Lincoln wear a distinctive apparel dating back to medieval times. It was revived early in the 20th century by

Precentor Wakeford, and consists of a white alb, over which is worn a black grey-edged cope. The junior choristers, 16 in number, are known as Burghersh Chanters, after Bishop Burghersh (1320–40). The present Cathedral School, where the choristers are educated, is a preparatory school for boys between the ages of 7 and 13. In my time choristers went to Lincoln School, where they could stay until they were 18. This meant that they could remain at the school after their voices had broken and they had left the choir. Some boys preserved their voices until long after the normal changing period, by which they attained a greater maturity in their singing, and developed a full and beautiful tone of a volume rarely heard today. I remember two of the boys being at least six feet in height, and they made a splendid sight as they led the procession, even if they did dwarf the rest of the choir.

The Dean of Lincoln, Dr Thomas Charles Fry, a former Headmaster of Berkhamsted School (1888–1910), was an octogenarian with a white patriarchal beard and a bald head. He was a small man, and had – as I vividly recall – astonishingly blue eyes, set disarmingly in a smooth pink face. He brought to his office as Dean that same stern discipline he had exercised as a public school headmaster, and he was a forceful character in every way. He was described by Derek Winterbottom in a biography of Fry as a 'Christian Socialist to whom the lay clerks of Lincoln stood and bowed while he passed by without acknowledgement'. He objected strongly to smoking, and visitors to the Deanery were informed that, if they insisted on smoking, a room was set aside for that purpose.

He was entirely unmusical, and went as far to say that music, being merely incidental, was not really necessary to worship. This led him into conflict with Dr Bennett, with whom he was not on speaking terms for many years, communicating only by note. But he had a passionate devotion to his lovely Minster, and when funds were urgently required for its restoration he made worldwide appeals. At the end of his life he bravely undertook an exhausting fundraising tour abroad, which proved too much for his advanced age, and from which he never recovered. He died in 1930, and I sang at his funeral. He had been Dean for 20 years.

It was at Lincoln that I was ticked-off by a tightly-gaitered Archdeacon for wearing plus-fours, a comfortable knickerbocker type of trousers then much in vogue. They were made to hang four inches below the knee, hence their name. Their capacious bagginess was often a target for rude remarks by small boys, and an apocryphal story was that centuries ago they had been invented by the Turks in expectation that a great prophet would be born suddenly of a man. I often wonder what the staid cathedral dignitaries of the past would have thought of the casual garb and long hair of the modern choirman. But in any case, and in any age, a cassock can always cover a multitude of sins.

My lay vicar colleagues were all splendid men, with a majority from Yorkshire. Out of a full complement of nine men, five had originated from the great choir at Leeds Parish Church, and myself from Sheffield. At one time Yorkshire supplied very many singers to cathedrals, and it is said that when Charles Hylton Stewart was appointed organist of Rochester Cathedral he greeted his new lay clerks by saying how glad he was to meet 'you men of Kent'. One of them replied: 'Eh, lad, we all come from Yorkshire'.

The bass line at Lincoln was supplied by Endersby, Woodward and Lofthouse, and while the two latter were excellent baritones, Lewis (Bill) Endersby stood out as a stupendous basso-profundo, the type of voice which seems to have completely disappeared. He was a handsome, commanding figure, and he could sing a bottom A flat or even a G *below* the stave with ease. When the mood took him he would sing the bass part in hymns an octave lower than written, producing an intriguing contra-fagotto effect.

An amusing reference to Endersby once appeared in an article in *Punch*, by Basil Boothroyd, who had once been a choirboy at Lincoln. During an Evensong Boothroyd said to Endersby: ' "What have you got on your hair?" His sleekness had caught the corner of my eye as we rose from the First Lesson, and old Bennett had begun a preliminary punishing of the keys. We were experts at the hushed aside. "Cat-muck and weasel pee", said Mr Endersby, breathing in deep for "My soul doth magnify the Lord, and my spirit hath rejoiced ..." It would have been an awful shock for my father.'[1]

Boyce's great anthem *O where shall wisdom be found?* was always given special treatment by Endersby and Dr Bennett. The passage which contains the words 'and a way for the lightning and the thunder' was the signal for a tremendous roar from Endersby,

[1] 'Father of the man', *Punch*, 18 September 1968, p 396.

answered by a great rumble of thunder from the organ, particularly the cavernous 32-ft pedal. In the past century John Goss was producing the same effects at St Paul's Cathedral. According to E J Hopkins, 'Whenever there occurred any reference to storm and tempests the organ used to give forth a deep roll'. It is curious how the dramatic sentiment of words and music can invoke involuntary and spontaneous reactions in some performers, which cannot always be dismissed as mere naivety or exhibitionism, comical though the effects may be. There was a notable occasion only a few years ago in one of our most famous choirs, when during the performance of this particular anthem a well-known lay vicar was so carried away that he shook the choir stalls vigorously and flashed the desk lights in and out to heighten the thunder-and-lightening effects. He told me afterwards that his actions were quite involuntary, but I noticed the twinkle in his eye... I heard the late Sidney Campbell, Organist of St George's Chapel, Windsor, most unpredictably play a completely extempore accompaniment to this anthem, including a stylistic ornamentation typical to accompaniments of that period. He too said he had been 'carried away'. But it nearly 'threw' the choir!

I much enjoyed singing with Endersby, particularly at concerts and dinners as a member of 'The Lincoln Minster Trio', of which Gavin Kay was not only the excellent tenor but also a virtuoso solo pianist and accompanist. He would transpose accompaniments to suit the phenomenal profundities of Endersby, who, when the audience clamoured for the song *Drinking*, for which he was famous, would oblige by singing it in the key of A flat, which involved starting on a bottom E flat!

John B Render, the appropriately named senior lay vicar, was a tenor, and he had been in the choir for 50 years. He was an accomplished musician and played several instruments. At a dinner given in his honour, Dr Bennett said he had never known him to make a mistake. Render corrected him, acknowledging, 'I made two'. He had difficulty in getting dentures to fit satisfactorily, so he carried a spare set or two in his cassock pocket – just in case. (I remember a lay clerk at Chester who regularly took out his teeth during services, and tapped them very audibly with a tin of denture fixative!)

John Render was married three times, and at Evensong on the day he returned from his third honeymoon, the anthem might well have been chosen for the occasion. It was *This is the record of John*, by

Gibbons, in which Render sang the solo. This anthem was for many years assigned to a tenor voice. It has been re-edited, and is now sung by an alto. The title also appears to have been updated, as it is often referred to as 'Jack's Disc'.

Fred Booth, retund and ruddy, was a noted bassoon player as well as a fine tenor. He was responsible for seeing that choirboys were properly robed, and no unbuttoned cassock, surplice awry or unbrushed hair escaped his eagle eye. He sang beautifully into his eighties.

Arthur Farrar and Tom Laidler were my alto colleagues, and they were both accomplished singers and highly experienced musicians. Farrar, a friendly though outspoken little Yorkshireman, would liven up a practice when he and Dr Bennett didn't quite see eye to eye, perhaps on some technical point. He kept poultry, and the number of eggs they produced was entered up daily on the Cathedral service sheets, which might read something like this: Anthem − *I sat down under His shadow* (6 pullets).

The assistant organist, E F R Woolley, discovered I was fond of cats, and he took me to see a retired bishop, who owned no fewer than ten magnificent specimens. They were all pedigreed, purring, prelate-like pussies, such as one would expect to find in exalted ecclesiastical circles. The good bishop had called them all by biblical names; and after rounding them up, I was formerly presented to each in turn: Ruth, Naomi, Jacob, Esau, Solomon, and so on. I paid due homage as I bent to shake paws, and I felt they approved. It has been implied − no doubt in jest (?) − that altos have an affinity with cats, probably because the animal is said to purr in falsetto, or uses the edges of his vocal chords, or whatever mechanism he has constituting a larynx. I have often wondered why so many men talk to cats in falsetto.

After morning service each day, lay vicars would hurtle down Steep Hill to Boots Cafe for coffee, a resources-stretching luxury in those days. There was an added attraction provided by a small string orchestra offering a little light relief from the Tallis, Byrd or Gibbons still ringing in our ears. One morning, as we were contentedly sipping, siphoning, slurping, gulping or gargling our coffee, according to the degree of refinement (or lack of it) in our drinking habits, the cafe door opened, and quite unexpectedly in walked Dr Bennett. The violinist, looking rather shocked at the unusual intrusion of the city's leading musician, brought the music to what sounded like an apologetic close. But the Doctor was equal to the occasion, and he called out: 'I say, what was that jolly piece you were playing?' '*You're the cream in my coffee*, sir', the violinist replied nervously. 'Well', said the Doctor, 'let's have it again, and thanks for the compliment'.

One of my great joys was to climb the 365 winding steps to the top of the Cathedral's central tower, from which there are panoramic views into the far distances. At that time the Cathedral was undergoing urgent restoration, and I remember a crack in the tower masonry which was wide enough for me to stand in. On my way up the tower, I always paused at the belfry, and timed it so that I could watch the celebrated 5½-ton bell — Great Tom — strike the hour. Having spent a lifetime with bells, and also living with them at close range, I prefer their enchantment at a distance. But to hear Lincoln's 12 magnificent bells from any distance is unforgettable. Few sounds are more evocative than bells, with their power to stir emotions of joy or grief, triumph, alarm or relief, to say nothing of that twinge of conscience they bring to many a lapsed churchgoer.

I had been at Lincoln less than two years when an alto vacancy occurred at Lichfield Cathedral. Although I was happy at Lincoln, my colleagues urged me to apply for the post, as in the 1930s Lichfield was a 'plum' among cathedral appointments. It carried the princely stipend of £180 per annum (then considered a living wage — I was paid £150 at Lincoln and £100 at Tenbury), and at that time there was no better paid layclerkship in the country. It had the added attraction of being a freehold or life appointment, which provided an unassailable security, and a vicar choral could only be removed from office for the gravest cause. As one of the most sought-after appointments, Lichfield had always been able to boast of many outstanding singers. I was the youngest of 50 applicants, from which a shortlist of ten was drawn up. After the final voice trial, which was a very searching one conducted by the organist, Ambrose Porter, and at which, in addition to a solo of my own choice, the set test-piece was *Slumber, beloved*, from Bach's *Christmas Oratorio*, I was summoned to the Chapter House to face the whole of the Cathedral body: Dean and Canons, Organist, and the Corporation of Vicars Choral, all of whom had a vote in the appointment. The Dean, Dr E H Savage, after offering me the post, leaned across the table and said to me very seriously: 'We have, however, only one thing against you (my heart sank), and that is your age, but believe me', he went on with a wry grin, 'that will improve'. He was right, and more than 60 years later I am hoping for further improvement!

Leaving Lincoln was a wrench. The Minster bells were ringing the night I went away from the city for the last time, and they sounded nostalgically reproachful, as if calling me to stay. As my train pulled out of the station, the sight of those radiant towers, bathed in moonlight and poised high over the city, as if they were suspended in the sky, etched a picture which could never be forgotten.

My successor at Lincoln was John Leslie Ramsay, a fine alto from Ely. We had much in common: we both wore plus-fours and we both rode motorbikes. However, John eventually left me to my more secular ways, for in 1955 he was ordained. Most of his ministry has been in the diocese of Lincoln.

CHAPTER FOUR

Lichfield and its continuing past

According to legend, the name Lichfield means 'field of the dead'. It was said that this had a special significance and referred to the massacre of Christians by Roman soldiers at the time of the Diocletian persecution. To this day we see in the city coat of arms 'an escutcheon of landscape with many martyrs in it several ways massacred'. This 'anciente and loyale citie of Lichfield' can claim many illustrious sons, such as Dr Johnson, Garrick, Addison and Erasmus Darwin, and a host of others who have achieved eminence in their respective fields. D L Murray wrote of Lichfield as follows:

> Nowhere in England does the past continue, preserving neither in amber nor in museum, but beating with the pulse of today. It is not content to 'survive': it must ever put forth green shoots. This is peculiarly true of Lichfield, where the visitor might be tempted to say that 1300 years of English history lie embalmed, if it were not for the vivid life that still bustles through its streets. It is to this moated quadrangle, where every stone and brick, every foot of soil is steeped in the essence of England, that the visitor finds his feet again and again lured back, from the dusky church of St Michael on its steep pre-Christian burial mound, whence Lichfield ('the field of the dead') was thought to draw its name, and its reason for existing, from venerable St Chad's across the field, with its holy well, commemorating the founder of the diocese; from the Guildhall, rich with its massive city plate; from Market Square, and Samuel Johnson's birthplace, so untouched by the tooth of time, that it seems that the clumsy schoolboy with his load of books, might issue at any moment from the door; from admiring so many comely Georgian houses, with their pillared porticos, still breathing the serenity of Augustan England, and peeping into the courtyards of so many ancient inns, where the blast of the coach horn, and the clatter of post-horses, seem barely silenced yet – he is always brought back to the Close and Cathedral.[1]

Johnson described Lichfield as a 'city of philosophers, the most sober, decent people in England: the genteelest in proportion to their wealth, and spoke the purest English'. This would be contradictory to a remark

[1] The *750th Anniversary of Lichfield Cathedral*, Programme of festival, 1946, p 4.

he once made to Boswell to the effect that all decent citizens of Lichfield got drunk every night. As pointed out by J L Clifford, allowing for Johnson's inconsistencies the term sober can only in this context refer to their characteristics.[2] But when I first came to Lichfield in the early 1930s, there was still a decided hangover from the 18th century in terms of alcoholic consumption, for there were (speaking from memory) over 60 pubs to a population of just over 8,000. All had regulars, and certainly appeared to thrive. Two out of an original number of five breweries still survived, and provided seemingly secure employment for many citizens.

After the initial shock of discovering that I was a strict teetotaller, my colleagues and all the rest of the populace with whom I came into contact, amongst whom I was to live on the best terms for many years, gradually came to accept my peculiarity in this respect. I was to sing at numerous dinners at local hotels and pubs, and as I raised my glass of lemonade, orange or grapefruit on a level with the foaming tankards all around me, the conviviality remained unimpaired by my abstemiousness, which says much for Dr Johnson's citizenly decency. Daniel Defoe also admired Lichfield, describing it as 'a place of good company, beyond all other towns in this or the neighbouring counties of Warwick and Derby'.

After the splendid spaciousness of Lincoln Cathedral, it took me some time to adjust to the relatively small compactness of Lichfield. But I was soon captivated by its delicate charm. Its three spires, the most beautiful group in the country, have been known affectionately for centuries as the 'Ladies of the Vale', and they rise with especial grace above the city, to command it and its pastoral landscape. There is no more beautiful stained glass in England than that of the Flemish Herckenrode Windows in the Lady Chapel, and I have never failed to pause wonderingly at the miraculously life-like monument of the 'Sleeping Children', Chantrey's masterpiece, given in 1817. As I gaze, my father's words come back to me: 'If you look closely, you can imagine they are breathing.'

The history of the cathedral arouses an endearing compassion, for no English cathedral has suffered so much at the hands of the desecrators. The Civil War of the 17th century saw Roundhead troops (described as 'the worst enemy the Cathedral had ever known')

[2] *The Young Samuel Johnson*, London, 1955.

let loose to profane the building with every conceivable and un-mentionable excess. Monuments were defaced, stained glass smashed, carved woodwork hewn down, and valuable records detroyed. Restoration under Wyatt, Gilbert Scott, and the Tractarian Revival went on until the end of the 19th century, and has come in for severe criticism, much of it quite unjustified:

Professor Edward S Prior described the interior as 'offensive to taste, for the same reason that the china reproductions of the Venus of Milo, or the oleographs of the Sistine Madonna were offensive to taste'.[3]

The restorers are castigated for choosing to reconstruct rather than repair. Britton's monograph of 1820 revealed a building of considerable magnificence in a terribly sad state of damage and decay. The restoration of the West Front was completed in 1884, and the canopied statues of saints and kings have been condemned as 'Victorian banalities', and 'moonfaced puppets'. But beauty must for ever lie in the eye of the beholder, and I am only one of the multitudes who have appreciated the merits of that West Front, which are all the more remarkable for being the work of Bridgeman, a local sculptor of note. For this lady of cathedrals to have emerged so gracefully from major surgery, with her scars so cleverly concealed, was a triumph for the devotion and dedication of all who toiled and prayed for her recovery.

It was the custom for newly elected vicars choral to serve one week's probation before the appointment was finally confirmed. This may seem a very short probation indeed, but it was an intensive one, and the week consisted of 14 choral services, at which I had to sing a solo or verse part at every service. My performances were carefully noted and recorded by every vicar choral, who had to sign a declaration of approval at the end of the week. At the ceremony of Installation, I was assigned to the stall of Sandiacre, a Prebendal stall, 'with all its rights and appurtenances', though thereafter I always sang, of course, in the lay vicars' stalls.

The Corporation of Vicars Choral, known as the Old Foundation, was an autonomous body of priest and lay vicars which had existed for over 800 years, until it was finally dissolved by an Order in Council under the Cathedral Measures Act of 1931, which also affected

[3] *The Cathedral Builders in England* (The Portfolio, Monographs on Artistic Subjects, No 46, November 1905), London, 1905, p 16.

other cathedrals such as St Paul's and Wells. I had the distinction of being the last lay vicar to be appointed under the Old Foundation, at the dissolution of which existing vicars choral retained their individual freeholds.

Some quaint customs had survived from the Middle Ages. 'Commons' was paid monthly at the rate of three pence per day, and was known as 'beer money', though it was originally intended to include bread and cheese. An interesting relic relating to 'Commons' which has survived is a glass goblet, or rummer, which used to be known as the 'Loving Cup', in which beer was passed round the lay vicars after services. It dates from 1720, and in 1950 was valued at £120, though it would of course be worth considerably more today. The cup was formerly kept in the possession of the senior lay vicar in his own home, and Herbert Parker was the last to do so; I remember seeing it in a china cabinet in his sitting room. He told me he shared his predecessors' constant anxiety for its safety, and the fear that it might meet with an accident. Dean Ironmonger managed to persuade the lay vicars to hand the cup over to the custody of the Dean and Chapter in 1950, when it was placed in a showcase in the cathedral, where it can still be seen in the nave.[4]

A medieval benefactor had also bequeathed two loaves to each vicar choral, to be distributed annually on St Thomas's Day, 21st December. In my early days the loaves were quite sizeable, but 20 years later they had shrunk to two bread rolls!

Another curious custom was the penalising of lay vicars who arrived late for services by fining them sixpence, later increased to half-a-crown. A not very effective deterrent, this custom was abandoned after the Second World War. Fines were recorded in a register of attendance known as the 'Intimator's Book', which was kept in turn annually by each lay vicar. One who was unpunctual needed to be particularly careful to remember what day it was in the church's calendar, so that he would be wearing the right-coloured cassock. It was not unknown for a latecomer, according to temperament, either to walk boldly through the choir screen, in full view, or creep stealthily

---

[4] It is of interest to note that in 1985, at the instigation of Raymond Leang, the senior lay vicar, the custom of drinking from the Loving Cup was revived after 200 years. The cup was taken to the King's Head Hotel, Lichfield, and filled with beer, and passed round the lay vicars. It was then replaced in its showcase in the Cathedral. It is intended to repeat this ancient custom once a year.

through a gate in the choir aisle in a purple cassock when he should have been wearing red, or vice-versa.

Late entries always evoked more than a *sotto voce* titter, and there is an amusing story of how one latecomer, in the wrong cassock, was greeted by a stage whisper: 'Who does he think he is — the goalkeeper?' (I once witnessed the amazing sight of three canons of Windsor in their usual murrey cassocks, flapping at speed back to their houses just before service on the first day of Advent, when they should have been wearing black!)

Lay vicars were at that time responsible for the laundering of their own surplices, with no specific regulation as to how often this should be done. This produced a variety of shades of cleanliness, from snow-white to the off-white, and in one notable case a surplice which had great brown snuff stains permanently streaked down its front. Snuff-taking was then very prevalent in Lichfield, and on one occasion I was temporarily blinded by it as it wafted down through a procession.

The capitular Body of Lichfield Cathedral consists of a dean and four residentiary canons. The Dean, Dr E H Savage — a former vicar of Halifax — was a noted scholar and authority on medieval manuscripts. An octogenarian and a widower, he was fond of his pipe and his garden. I was chatting to him one day when he took his pipe from his mouth and said: 'I make special journeys to Derby (24 miles) to buy these pipes. This is my favourite and cost 15 pence' (the old one shilling and three pence). He would attend morning services on Christmas Day, after which he would lock himself up in solitude to meditate on departed loved ones, notably his wife, who had died in childbirth. He was strongly opposed to publicising cathedral services in any form, particularly by broadcasting, and it was ironic that he was to be succeeded by a famous broadcaster. Once after Matins, with not a single soul in the congregation, he said to the choir: 'Thank you all for singing so beautifully to an empty cathedral: you were really singing to God this morning'.

The residentiary canons were Moncrief, Penny, Bright and Stockley. Canon Penny was undoubtedly the real 'character' of the Chapter. A nonagenarian, he was a former Rector of Wolverhampton. He was a big, heavy man with a great booming voice, and he walked splay-footed with a stick. His daughter, Dora (later Mrs Richard Powell), was the immortal 'Dorabella' of Elgar's *Enigma Variations*. He was noted for his loud and caustic comments during services, and at

[37]

Evensong one day the final notes of Stanford's anthem *The Lord is my Shepherd* had hardly died away when he banged the floor of his stall with his stick, and boomed: 'I've never heard it before, and I don't want to hear it again.'

An annual highlight in the music list was the bass duet *The Lord is a man of war*, from Handel's *Israel in Egypt*, which never enjoyed less than the best treatment from Herbert Parker and James Coleman. Generations of choirboys loved it, and it was always recalled at Old Choristers' dinners. Coleman would cross over from the Cantoris side to Decani to join Parker for this anthem, and the sight and sound of those two together could never be forgotten. Parker, five feet nothing, was completely dwarfed by the massive Coleman, and as they took their stance everyone held his breath. Parker would lead off with a tremendous *The Lord is a man of war*, running up to a superb top E. There was something about that entry from the mighty little York-shireman which said unmistakeably, 'let t'battle commence'. Coleman would match that entry, and soon the two were locked in deadly combat, and the stalls shook. One felt that Pharaoh's chariots and his hosts had truly been cast into the sea, and the chosen captains drowned. It was really thrilling to hear, though it once raised this comment from the unmusical Canon Penny: 'Yes, it was wonderful, but perhaps more wonderful than beautiful, and in any case – who won?'

A famous story about Canon Penny grew out of an incident which occurred at Evensong one hot summer day, and of which I was a witness. The Dean was not feeling well enough to read the second lesson, so he sent Billy Dodd, the Head Verger, across to Canon Penny's stall to ask him to read the lesson. 'Tell him I can't', he snorted loudly ... 'I've taken my boots off!' Penny disliked motor cars, and I once saw him give a parked car a thwack with his stick. He turned to me and said: 'I hate the damned things.' He always journeyed around the city by pony and trap.

Of the priest vicars (Bradley, Hardy, Cresswell and Ashworth), the most remarkable was the aged Bradley, known to generations of choir-boys as 'bogo' (or sometimes 'Gobo') for some unknown reasons. He was a bachelor whose early life was something of a mystery and a subject on which he could not be drawn. He would not divulge his age, but he had been at Lichfield for well over 50 years, which made him at least over 80, or more likely beyond that age, judging from his appearance. When I first saw him I was intrigued by his caricature-like figure. He always wore a cassock and carried an umbrella, but it was his face which was so startling. He was completely hairless, and his skin was like yellow parchment, which gave him a deathly, mask-like look. He was a noted Latin scholar, and meticulous in the care of the books in his stall, which he had bound himself in red velvet.

He was Choristers' Chaplain, and the late Evan Slater, a former chorister, who was for many years Secretary of the Old Choristers' Association, recalls how he would greet each boy before service by shaking hands. But any boy who dared to touch any of the Cathedral stonework was severely reprimanded, and would have his hand slapped. Boys used to do this 'just for devilment', I am told. He would write the following in choristers' autograph albums: 'Never say die, never tell a lie, never put a finger in another person's pie.' He had certain idiosyncracies in his articulation, with a curious hissing of sibilants. He could still intone well, but his 'O Lord, open thou our lips-s-s-s' was often the signal for some members of the choir for an unkind hissing response: 'and our mouth shall show forth Thy prais-s-s-se'.

The aura of mystery surrounding him was heightened by the generally accepted belief that he was the original Mad Hatter in *Alice in Wonderland*. An account of his death and funeral in 1931, which appeared in *The Lichfield Mercury*, gave support to what I have always understood to be correct:

> There is probably some solid foundation from the story which has always been accepted without question that it was on him that the Rev C L Dodgson (Lewis Carroll) based the character of the Mad Hatter in *Alice in Wonderland*, and he was also said to have been the prototype of the Reverend Spalding in *The Private Secretary*.

Contemporary drawings of the Mad Hatter quite definitely remind one of what a younger Bradley might have been, his features remarkable on account of his curved nose. When he was questioned about his legendary connection with Dodgson, Bradley would terminate the conversation, saying: 'He was-s-s such a naughty man' and immediately shuffle away. There were, of course, other contenders for the title of Mad Hatter, but those who knew Bradley will ever see him as having been ideal for the role.[5]

[5] It is possible that Edward Bradley (kinsman of a Dean of Westminster), as a student of Wadham College, might have attended Dodgson's tutorials in mathematics. But he was not in residence in 1865 when *Alice in Wonderland* was published. He graduated as BA in 1872 – the year of *Through the Looking-Glass* – and became Deputy Priest Vicar of Lichfield in 1883.

CHAPTER FIVE
The musicians of Lichfield

There were three alto, three tenor, and three bass lay vicars at Lichfield, who, while holding their appointments for life, had to provide deputies when, either through age or infirmity, they were no longer capable of sustaining their part. Until 1939 Lichfield was justly proud that it maintained two choral services daily (without any break) for the 365 days of the year, which was said to have been unique. To achieve this, holidays had to be staggered by members of the choir, and great use was made of services for men's voices during the normal holiday periods, so that a choir was always on duty.

The choir school consisted mainly of local boys, and a few specially selected boarders from other parts of the country; chorister-ships were highly competitive. The education of the choristers was in the hands of Charles Bailey, who worked wonders in spite of the widely differing age-range of the boys. This school, which had for its motto the words 'Serve God and be cheerful' (which is still to be seen over the door of the old school in Dam Street), was closed in 1941. It was replaced by St Chad's Cathedral School, established by the Dean and Chapter as a preparatory school for fee-paying boarders, which now occupies the former Bishop's Palace in the Close. My son John later entered the new school, and those fathers who are fortunate enough to have their sons singing with them in the same choir, know what a joy that can be. My younger son Christopher was a chorister at Eton College, and I always welcomed an opportunity to sing in the choir when he was there.[1]

[1] Founded by Henry VI in 1443, as a sister foundation for King's College, Cambridge, Eton College had a trained choir of 16 choristers and 10 clerks from the beginning. *The Eton Choirbook* (modern edition *Musica Britannica*, vols 10 (1956) and XI (1958), is one of the most famous of all collections of church music, and contains masterpieces from the late 15th century. Many distinguished musicians have served as Precentor of Eton in recent times, and when the choral foundation was abolished – as an 'economy' measure in 1968 – there was general dismay and vigorous opposition. A service in which the combined choirs of Eton, King's Winchester and New (Oxford) Colleges took part was held to mark the sad end of a great tradition.

Choristers of Lichfield have reached eminence in many walks of life, and the school has produced musicians of note, among them Richard Lloyd, organist of Durham Cathedral, and John Turner, of Glasgow Cathedral.

Ambrose Porter, the Cathedral organist, was an exceptional trainer of boys' voices. He was a firm believer in 'full head resonation', which developed the kind of tone capable of filling a large building with magnificent effect.

Revolutionary changes in the training of boys' voices are now becoming all too apparent in certain choirs, and are bound up with what has been described by Cecil Clutton as a 'return to a simple, virile kind of organ accompaniment consistent with a Church which increasingly sheds false sentiment (?), and hand-in-hand with these trends goes a return to a more virile, less eviscerated kind of singing, especially by boys.'[2]

George Malcolm, in an article entitled 'Boys' Voices', which appeared some years ago in *The Preparatory Schools' Review*, says

> In foreign countries, it is considered perfectly possible to train a boy's voice, to refine it, and develop it into a medium of real musical beauty, without destroying its natural timbre, and without removing from it the characteristics of the normal human boy. Yet in England, most choirboys are systematically trained to produce an artificial and quite unnatural sound, popularly known as 'Cathedral tone'. Certainly the tone is pure if purity connotes only the negative emasculated quality of an Angel on a Christmas Card; but if it means, if by any chance it means positive upstanding integrity of early youth, then this pretty fluting sound is an insult to boyhood.

Here we have what can only be regarded as a serious challenge to that unique quality of English choirboy tone which stood the test of centuries, and became the envy of the world. It was seen at its very finest in such voices as that of Ernest Lough, who achieved celebrity in the recording made over 60 years ago of Mendelssohn's *Hear my prayer (O for the wings of a dove)*. The kind of tone he epitomised was to be heard for so many years at the Temple Church.

Dr Walter S Vale, a celebrated trainer of choirboys at All Saints, Margaret Street, London, said in his *Training of Boys' Voices*:

> With its many disadvantages, the average boy's voice has one great asset, its purity. The flute-like quality of the boy's so-called head voice closely

---

[2] 'Recent Trends in British Organ-building', in *English Church Music* (RSCM, 1963).

resembled what is probably the purest musical sound, the noise of the tuning fork, and if, when this quality is carried down to say G or F and lower, we combine with it a certain quality like that of the fiddle G string, we have a very beautiful musical sound.

Despite what may be thought to the contrary by proponents of an open, edgy tone in boys' voices, who are apt to dismiss the traditional head voice derisively and unjustly as the 'Anglican coo', the treble voice remains essentially a head voice, dependent on full head resonation for any degree of amplification and ringing quality. To remove a boy's voice from his head by systematically training it upwards to induce an edge, is to place it inevitably in the chest and throat. By thus raising the larynx and constricting the throat spaces we have what used to be known as 'Continental tone' (perhaps it should now be updated and called 'Common Market tone'). It is already being discovered that this type of singing, which has its counterpart in the incisive edge in many adult voices of today, notably among counter-tenors, is as much responsible for the premature termination of a boy's singing career as the fact that the boys are now reaching physical maturity earlier. In this gimmick-ridden age we should mourn the moribund art of *bel canto,* and pray for its revival.[3]

The type of treble singing produced by Ambrose Porter was free of gimmicks, and his choir training was persuasive rather than forceful. A former assistant of Gloucester Cathedral to Sir Herbert Brewer, he was a product of a school of musicians who graduated from the organ lofts of this country, well equipped in virtually every aspect of English church music. After some years as organist of St Matthias' Church, Richmond, Surrey, Porter succeeded John B Lott at Lichfield in 1925, where it soon became apparent that he was a musician of outstanding quality. He remained at Lichfield until he retired in 1959, at the age of 74. He achieved a national reputation as a recitalist and

---

[3] The recent introduction of girls' choirs into cathedrals raises the controversial question as to whether they are a welcome innovation or an encroachment into a domain where all-male choirs have been an exclusive preserve for many centuries. Girl choristers in cathedrals have the same advantages as boys in receiving a first-class training in voice production and technique. But however excellently they can be taught to sing, it remains indisputable that nothing can equal the unique purity of tone and robustness of boys' voices, imparting that characteristic timbre which has always been the hallmark of the English Cathedral Choir. Girls' choirs sing with enthusiasm, and make a commendable contribution to the worship of God. But where they coexist with boys choirs in cathedrals they should remain and function as separate entities.

broadcaster, and there were few who were so accompaniment. He was also a magnificent pianist.

The fact that he was content to stay at Lichfield so long was typical of one who was completely dedicated to his cathedral. He was immensely proud of his superb Hill organ, which was restored in 1974 by Hill, Norman and Beard, under the guidance of his successor, Richard Greening, whom I came to know when he was assistant organist of St George's Chapel, Windsor. Ambrose Porter was shy and retiring, but he had great charm, and it was a pleasure and privilege to work with him. He died in 1971, at the age of 85. A notable assistant organist to Ambrose Porter for 20 years was Edgar Morgan. He was Director of Music at King Edward VI School at Lichfield, organist of Walsall Parish Church and Chorus Master at the BBC in Birmingham. He was a diminutive figure, only 5 feet 2 inches in height, and he wore immaculate suits and a bowler hat. He had a large 'Rover 75' car, and he was so short that only his bowler hat and wash leather gloves on the steering wheel were visible as he drove by!

In recalling my colleagues at Lichfield, I see before me a collection of some of the most remarkable men it would be possible to meet in any choir: each one a virtuoso singer, each one in his way a character, and most having held cathedral appointments elsewhere. I had succeeded Samuel Hase, who died at 46, and my alto colleagues were Enoch Richardson and William Milne Wood, both of whom were lay clerks at Christ Church, Oxford, under Charles Harford Lloyd. I never actually sang with Richardson, who had a great reputation, as he was in his 70s and an invalid. But he had a deputy to sing for him, George Knight, who developed a fine voice, and was eventually appointed a lay vicar choral. Richardson was succeeded by Hubert Appleyard, of Wells, an excellent musician, who was City Librarian for many years.

Although I only sang with William Wood for a short time, it was a memorable experience. He was a refined, charming man, with a truly splendid voice, a genuine countertenor, ie, a one-register voice of high tenor timbre, which he retained into old age. There was an immediate rapport between us, and I missed him sadly after his death. He was noted for his singing of Mendelsohn's *O rest in the Lord*, and those words appear on his gravestone in St Michael's Churchyard.

Whenever I visit Lichfield I always make a pilgrimage to his grave, and one such visit stands out in my memory. It was a beautiful day in May, and the huge churchyard was completely deserted. As I stood in silent contemplation, the words 'O rest in the Lord' met my eyes. I seemed to be aware of his presence, and quite unconsciously I found myself singing that solo which I continued to the end, to a lovely birdsong accompaniment. Such moments in a lifetime are to be cherished, and are far more spiritual than merely mawkishly sentimental.

The tenors were Harold Hall, Roland Cook and Albert Hodkinson. Hall had an operatic type of voice of tremendous power, while Hodkinson produced a contrast with a light tenor of remarkable range. His brother Charles, a former Lichfield Cathedral chorister, was a renowned bass of Chester Cathedral for many years. The singing of Roland Cook (formerly at Canterbury) has left abiding memories. He had a beautiful lyric tenor voice, and in this particular field he was considered to have few equals in the cathedral world. He was a member of the BBC Midland Singers, of which I later became a member. We were close friends, and fellow members with Hodkinson and Parker of the Lichfield Cathedral Quartet, which flourished for 20 years, broadcasting on many occasions.

The bass line in the choir in those days is now legendary, as all three were superlative singers. James Coleman, a Staffordshire man from West Bromwich, where he was venerated, as indeed he was throughout the Black Country, came to Lichfield from Southwell Minster in 1900. A heavy commanding physique gave him particular authority in his role of *Elijah*. His voice was a real basso-cantante, rich and voluminous, and his singing was refined and polished. He died suddenly on his way to the cathedral one Sunday morning in 1942. He was 66.

In describing Herbert Parker, I have to pause to consider how I could possibly do justice to one whose bass singing left an indelible impression on all who heard him. A Yorkshireman who had started his career as principal bass at Leeds Parish Church, he came to Lichfield in 1904. He was only about 5 feet 3 inches in height, but he had a huge torso and very short legs and tiny feet. He wore 19-inch collars! He was fond of relating his early days in the choir when his colleagues on the decani side were even shorter than he was. 'I was t'giant' he would chuckle.

In the whole of my singing career I can recall few voices which gave me a greater thrill. It was a truly majestic organ, with the incredible range of three octaves, from a top tenor A to A below the bass stave, and he had a brilliant technique. I have heard him referred to as the 'mighty atom', as it seemed amazing that such tone and volume could pour from so diminutive a figure. Sir Walford Davies described him as a 'Prince of cathedral basses', and wrote the title part in his *Everyman* with him in mind. The dramatic solo in Ernest Walker's male-voice anthem *Lord, Thou has been our refuge* was one of his many specialities and he could be guaranteed to give so intensely moving a performance that I have seen his colleagues, even the hard-boiled ones and clergy too, with tears in their eyes as he sang the concluding words of the solo, 'We bring our years to an end, as it were a tale that is told', in a beautifully executed *pianissimo*. But there was nothing maudlin or sentimental about his singing. It was sheer beauty of words and music interpreted through an outstanding medium. In the early days of broadcasting he was to be heard frequently from Savoy Hill.

We much enjoyed our common experiences, and as when we walked to and from the cathedral, or when travelling to engagements, he would reminisce fascinatingly on celebrities with whom he had sung. He gave me many valuable tips on singing, which as a youngster I was only too glad to have from such an old campaigner. For fun he would often lapse into Yorkshire dialect, and I have seen many an amused grin on the faces of passers-by when they heard old Herbert holding forth in his best 'Yorkshire' as his deep resonant voice rang out. Although he had always been able to command substantial fees for outside engagements, which took him frequently to London and all over the country, he had the professional's justifiable attitude that while one should always be willing to give one's services for a charitable cause, the labourer was worthy of his hire. With typical Yorkshire philosophy he would say: 'Remember, lad, if tha can sing for nowt, tha can stop at hooam for nowt!'

Herbert was a dog-lover, and his collie 'Duke' often accompanied him to the cathedral, and would wait outside the vestry until the service was over. But sometimes he would get impatient, or perhaps he wished to add his contribution to the singing, as Herbert had taught him to 'sing' a few notes, and he would set up a scalewise howl. Once, during the reading of a lesson, Herbert left his stall and went to the vestry door. When he came back he said loudly enough for everyone to hear: 'I've told him to shut up and be a good boy.' The service proceeded without further canine obbligato.

Herbert was proud of his Scottish wife, Christian Stobie Parker, sometime Headmistress of a local school, twice Mayor of Lichfield, and a distinguished civil and social worker. Herbert's singing remained unimpaired until the end of his life. I gave a recital with him at Keele University in 1953, when he gave a magnificent performance of Purcell's *They that go down to the sea in ships*, which has a notable solo which only a basso-profundo can attempt. He was then 78 years of age. He sang at the cathedral up to a few days before his death at the age of 81. I am only one who benefited greatly from knowing him, and I revere his memory.

The third bass was Arthur Wrigglesworth, yet another Yorkshireman from Leeds. He came to Lichfield from Chichester, and was an operatic type of baritone with an extended upper range. It was a splendid voice of a timbre strikingly similar to that of Dennis Noble.

My eulogies of the Lichfield vicars choral of yesterday may seem to be lavish, if not indeed exaggerated by the passage of time; yet they are corroborated by all who knew them in their day. Of such men is the whole fabric of the unique church music tradition of England constituted, and as they were so were countless others across the ages.

When I arrived at Lichfield the services still had something of a Victorian atmosphere. The lighting was by gas, and the brackets in the choir stalls had gas mantles which hissed and plopped (the aptly named manager of the Gas Company was Mr Mantle).

Victorian composers, much loved by Dean Savage, were still much in evidence on the service lists. But in spite of this the repertoire generally was extensive, as it needed to be with so many services. The better-known oratorios and various Bach cantatas – including *Wachet auf* und *Gottes Zeit ist die allerbeste Zeit* – were sung frequently. I remember being intrigued with the old-fashioned custom of intoning the General Confession, when each sentence was first sung by a Priest Vicar, and then repeated by the choir and congregation. It was pointed out to me that this was strictly in accordance with the bidding in the Prayer Book, where the prayer preceding the Confession ends with the words 'saying *after* me'. Responses by E G Monk, sung in the vestibule before and after services, were a notable feature.

A landmark in the history of Lichfield Cathedral was its 750th Anniversary Festival, celebrated with great pageantry in the presence of HM The Queen in June 1946. Because of the aftermath of war, the festival was held a year late, as the original work was begun on the first three pairs of arches east of the choir screen, the earliest part of the Cathedral in 1195. There was a variety of events, the highlight of which was a specially commissioned play by Dorothy Sayers, *The Just Vengeance*, with a West End cast, and music by Antony Hopkins, then at the beginning of his career. The singing was provided by the Cathedral Choir and the Musical Society. In the introduction Dorothy Sayers wrote:

> In form, the drama is a miracle play of man's insufficiency and God's redemptive act, set against the background of contemporary crisis. The whole action takes place in the moment of the death of an airman shot down during the last war. In that moment his spirit finds itself drawn into the fellowship of his native city of Lichfield; there, being shown in an image the meaning of the Atonement, he accepts the cross, and passes in that act of choice, from the image to the reality.

Dorothy Sayers presented an unforgettable picture in her mannish tweeds, brogues and trilby hat. She never failed to make her presence felt. On arrival at the Cathedral door for the first performance of *The Just Vengeance*, she was asked for her ticket of admittance. 'Ticket?' she boomed ... 'out of my way, I wrote the damned thing!' The play had some extremely dramatic moments, particularly when George Fox, the Quaker, entering from the back of the Cathedral, Bible under his arm, shouted: 'Woe to the bloody city of Lichfield'. In his journal for 1651, Fox describes a vision he had when he saw the streets of Lichfield running in blood. The enacting of the Crucifixion by soldiers from the Upper Stage, with the actor Raf de la Torre as the Persona, with voice ringing out poignantly: 'Eloi, Eloi, Lama Sabacthani?' ('My God, My God, why hast Thou forsaken me?') was extremely moving.

Three hundred years after George Fox's denunciation of the city, Lichfield held its first festival of music and drama. No doubt this tercentenary was unintentional. Nevertheless, the festival of 1951 began with the powerful tragedy of T S Eliot's *Murder in the Cathedral*. The music was composed by Ambrose Porter, and the choral parts performed by the lay vicars and the local musical society. Dressed in a monkish habit, we found it somewhat unnerving to find our way along the darkened aisles. Somehow, our cathedrals seem to grow larger as the daylight fades, and at night they have an immensity of their own.

I had for many years other duties in Lichfield than those in the cathedral, for I served as choirmaster at St Michael's Church. When I took over that responsibility the Rector was Prebendary Percival Howard, an excellent parish priest but entirely unmusical. This, however, did not deter him from wishing to dictate the pace of hymns, all of which, whatever their sentiment, must go at a 'cracking pace and with a swing', and with a touch of finality he would add: 'and I'm boss'.

The organist was George Cooper, a dear old man who had been at the church for as long as anyone could remember. He was a good musician and a well-known music teacher, and he and I worked splendidly together. But with advancing years he began to go deaf, and the Rector would begin to grow impatient if he thought a hymn or psalm was dragging. 'Come on, George,' he would say, 'get a move on.' George, unheeding, continued at the same pace. The Rector, a bit louder: 'George, do you hear, quicker.' No response. In exasperation the Rector would then beat out the time loudly on the organ stool with his hand. I was only the choirmaster, but in such situations the choir would look to me for guidance, and I would give a gentle beat at the right tempo, which more often than not was the one George had been playing.

In spite of these contretemps, the Rector and I remained on good terms, and I had *carte blanche* as far as the training of the choir was concerned, for whatever he thought about hymns he knew that anthems and service were beyond his understanding.

It was a competent and loyal choir, which maintained a high standard for years. With the advent of a new Rector, the Rev Maurice Elrington, who was musical, the music flourished, and several festivals and recitals were held. After repeated requests, I agreed to a performance of Stainer's *Crucifixion*, and it was such a success, drawing capacity congregations, that it became an annual event. But there were the inevitable critics who remonstrated with me for putting on what one person described as 'banal Victorian rubbish'. Stainer is still maligned by some musicians (although a swing in favour of Victorian culture has diminished denigration of this work), and one of the most uncharitable of stories is about a professor of music who when asked the question 'What do you think of Stainer's *Crucifixion*?', he replied, 'I would be heartily in favour of it!' Whatever its merits or demerits, this simple work, which has the advantage of being within the scope of almost any choir, still has a powerful message and continues to draw the crowds. Most singers of whatever attainment usually enjoy it, and long may they continue to 'Fling wide the gates'.

I was always impressed by the enthusiasm of Staffordshire choirs, but on occasion local vowels would infiltrate, which could usually be overcome by some discreet patterning. But one Easter I was rehearsing Ley's *The Strife is o'er*, in which these words occur:

> Death's mightiest power have done their worst,
> And Jesus hath his foes dispersed;
> Let shout of praise and joy outburst: Alleluya!

Such a verse just could not avoid the best Staffordshire treatment, and to a man I got:

> Death's moightiest powers have done their wearst,
> And Jesus hath His fows dispearsed;
> lets shout of prise and jy outbearst: Olleluya!

They loved that verse, and really — I hadn't the heart.

My grandfather, Joshua Hodgson, distinctly remembered the local vernacular being used in his native Cleckheaton, Yorkshire, well over a century ago, viz:

> Jesus shall reign where ee're the soon
> Doth his successive journeys roon;
> His kingdom stretch from shooer to shooer,
> Till mooins shall wax and wane na moor.

CHAPTER SIX
Cathedral characters

Notoriously, the Church has always attracted oddities and eccentrics, and cathedral congregations in my experience seem to have had more than their fair share. I have always felt sympathetic to such people (are we not all 'odd' in some way or another?), and getting to know them can be a rewarding experience. I have known those who were mentally disturbed, and of them many have obviously gained great comfort and succour in the atmosphere of a church. But if they cannot find these there – where else? Sometimes they may invoke a quiet chuckle; yet they can remind us of our own quirks which too may provoke behind-the-back merriment.

One octogenarian spinster (an evocative, now virtually extinct, word) had been a regular attender at the cathedral for more than half a century. She dressed in black Victorian clothes and walked with mincing steps, holding up her skirt the while lest it trail in the dust. It was said by those of a romantic disposition that she had in youth been jilted by a nobleman. He had arranged to travel to Lichfield from afar to formulate wedding plans. But – so the story goes – he never turned up, and every day thereafter the poor little old lady was to be seen, skirt upheld, heading for Trent Valley Station 'to meet his Lordship'. Her lifelong association with the cathedral fostered in her a passion for church music and, laudable though that may be, it was centred round the tenor part, which in many well-known anthems and services she had learned off by heart. It may well be imagined that at her advanced age her larynx had curdled (as I have heard it described), and to the constant exasperation of the choir in general and the tenors in particular, she insisted on joining in with a rasping, penetrating croak. What made it worse was that she was often at least one beat ahead, particularly in leads, and she could beat the whole choir to it with an 'Ah-ah-me-en' at the end of prayers. Polite (and sometimes not so polite) remonstrations from vergers and others quietened her for a time. But when one of her favourites appeared on the list, the urge was too great, and once again she became the 'leading' tenor. Many a dull service has been livened up by Herbert Parker's dog, and the little lady in black.

Another dear old spinster, a Miss Crane, whose father had been an alto in the choir 50 years before, hardly ever missed a service. Afterwards she would wait for me, and pass the same remark, year in, year out: 'Thank you, I only come to hear the altos'.

An aristocratic and elegant old lady, a patient in a mental hospital, attended services accompanied by a nurse. She would hail me outside the cathedral, and beckon me with a deep loud voice: 'Do come heah, and sing to me, deah'.

One of the cathedral regulars was a retired telegraphist named Billy Hughes. He had a white beard, wore a battered bowler hat, and had his trousers braced half way up his legs. He walked with his head at an angle, which gave the impression from a distance that it was resting on his shoulder, his hat and his head forming a horizontal line. He talked to himself as he walked with his fox terrier, which he had on a lead so short that the poor animal had its neck up in the air. On more than one occasion I have seen Billy walking along after a visit to the butcher's, with a huge bone sticking gruesomely out of his pocket. He carried his spectacles in a large brown paper bag, and it was intriguing to watch him dive into its depths. An intelli,ent man, with a retentive memory, he had a fund of reminiscence; of vicars choral of 70 years before. He sang alto in St Chad's Church choir, and was very knowledgeable about church music. Whenever I met him he aired the same old grievance in his Staffordshire accent: 'I was the must underpaid man on God's airth ... forty-four years before I landed one hundred and ten pounds per annum.' Vergers had to keep a wary eye on him during services. He would sit in the nave, where in hot weather he was likely to take off his boots (which was no more than Canon Penny did!) and also his socks, and then lift his bare feet on top of the chair in front of him.

Another 'salubrious' memory is of an aged member of the cathedral clergy who was incontinent. He was a dear old man, and it was sad to see him dragging himself along the nave, leaving a tell-tale trail behind him. One of the vergers, an irreverent wag, would point down the nave after he had passed, and start humming the well-known old song *There's a long, long trail a-winding*!

Another local, named George, could often be seen in and around the cathedral. He was better known as 'Birdie' on account of his peculiar hopping gait. He wore a macintosh with a capacious pocket in which he carried an alarm clock. When one saw him, it was customary to whistle him, when he would stop dead in his hopping, turn around swiftly, and wait for the inevitable question: 'What time is it, George?' He would dive in his pocket and out came the clock, which he would hold up high, and then put it back and hop off without a word.

During service one winter's morning, the cathedral was deserted except for the choir, a Priest Vicar and a Canon, when a scrawny tabby cat came through the choir-screen howling piteously. The animal actually made an appropriate entry at the words 'O go your way into His gates' in the *Jubilate*. It jumped on to the stall occupied by Harold Hall, the tenor, and sat on his music desk, facing him with head cocked as he sang. With the rest of us Harold managed to choke his way to the end of the *Gloria*, when the cat jumped down and fled. Perhaps it was the reincarnation of one of those poor persecuted animals who 300 years before suffered diabolically at the hands of Roundhead soldiers, who organised cat-chases in the cathedral.

The vergers who stand out in my memory were Billy Dodd, Fred Bee, Len Smith, Percy Hill and Teddy Hart (later Head Verger at Exeter). They all loved their cathedral, and took pride in showing visitors around. There is an old story of a Lichfield verger whose loyalty to the cathedral allowed no criticism. On visiting York Minster he told a verger he came from Lichfield. He met with a haughty – 'Lichfield? We could put that inside here.' 'Aye, perhaps you could', came the reply, 'and would'nt it improve it.' Anna Seward (c.1742–1809), famous in 18th-century literary circles, and known as the 'Swan of Lichfield', also recorded a visit to York Minster: 'But if my sight perceived the undying superiority of York Minster, my ear acknowledged the yet more transcendent harmonic advantage of the Gothic boast of Lichfield'. Anna Seward was known to have had an illicit relationship with John Saville (1735–1803), who was married and lived in the Close. He was a famous Lichfield alto who was in great demand at concerts and festivals, including the Three Choirs Festival, appearing at Gloucester in 1790. His liaison with Anna Seward, which caused a scandal in the Close, lasted for more than thirty years until his death in 1803. He is immortalised in an epitaph written by Anna Seward, which may be seen on a tablet erected to his memory on the wall of the south transept of Lichfield Cathedral, which reads as follows:

Sacred to the Memory
of
JOHN SAVILLE

48 Years Vicar-Choral of this Cathedral.
Ob: Aug'sta. 2ndo 1803 AEta '67

Once in the Heart cold in yon narrow cell,
Did each mild grace, each ardent virtue dwell;
Kind and kind tears for other's want and woe.
For other's joy, the gratulating glow:
And skill to mark and eloquence to claim
For genius in each art, the palm of fame,
Ye choral Walls, ye lost the matchless song
When the last silence stiffen'd on that tongue
Ah! who may now your pealing anthems raise
In soul-pour'd tones of fervent prayer and praise?
Saville, thy lips, twice on thy final day,
Here breath'd, in health and hope the sacred lay;
Short pangs, ere night, their fatal signal gave,
Quench'd the bright Sun for thee — and op'd the Grave!
Now from that graceful form and beaming face
Insatiate worms the lingering likeness chase,
But thy pure Spirit fled from pains and fears
To sinless-changeless-everlasting Spheres.
Sleep then, pale mortal Frame, in yon low shrine
'Till Angels wake thee with a note like thine'.[1]

Dean Savage died in 1938, and was succeeded by the Rev Freddie Iremonger, a famous broadcaster. He was the first BBC Director of Religious Broadcasting, and was commentator in Westminster Abbey at the coronation in 1937.[2] He wore beautifully cut clothes, was a connoisseur of wines and food, and a fine preacher, whose reading of the lessons was impeccable. A rather autocratic bachelor, he spent most of his time at Lichfield writing the definitive biography of William Temple, Archbishop of Canterbury.

We also had a new Bishop in Edward Woods, who came with a national reputation as a broadcaster when Bishop of Croydon. He was a delightful man, and admired and respected by all. I got to know

[1] A full account of the life of John Saville of Lichfield appears in *The History and Technique of the Counter-Tenor* by Peter Giles (Scolar Press, 1995).
[2] The successor to Bishop Holderness, who retired as Dean in 1979, was J H Lang, who had also been BBC Director of Religious Broadcasting to the time of his Lichfield appointment.

him well, and we became good friends. He had a resonant and very distinctive speaking voice, which was a family characteristic inherited by his son, Robin Woods, who became Bishop of Worcester, whom I came to know when he was Dean of Windsor. The new Bishop and Dean soon had Lichfield Cathedral on the air and services were broadcast frequently.

As well as a Bishop and Dean of a new dispensation, there were also newcomers among the canons. Robert Hodson, Precentor and Archdeacon of Stafford, had been Rector of St Peter's Collegiate Church, Wolverhampton, and was well-known for his sense of humour and his ability to discountenance the pompous. He was not particularly musical, and the Dean had told him that a Precentor should be a musician, or, as he put it, 'a *proper* Precentor'. Archdeacon Hodson afterwards became Bishop of Shrewsbury, and I met him in the Close one day after a service at which he had been the visiting preacher. 'Freddy', he said, with a roguish grin, 'the Dean invited me to occupy the stall next to my old Precentor's stall this morning. I declined, very politely, of course, and said: "Surely, Mr Dean, you would not wish an improper Precentor to sit next to a *proper* Precentor?"'

Another residentiary canon was Lempriere Hammond, who had started life as an engineer, and later became Bishop of Stafford. His all-consuming passion was cricket, on which game he was something of an authority. It was amusing to see him walking in the street taking imaginary swipes at a cricket ball, or throwing up his hat and catching it. On meeting him it became a regular ritual for him to take up a batting stance, while the other person, often on the opposite side of the street, would swing an imaginary ball. As the invisible bat met the invisible ball, he would add a touch of reality by making a loud clicking noise with his tongue. At that time the Yorkshire cricketer Hedley Verity (killed in the Sicily campaign) was at the height of his fame, and when the words in Psalm 111, 'the works of his hands are *verity* and judgement' were being sung, he would exchange a knowing grin with the lay vicars.[3]

One of my colleagues was given to burlesquing the Psalms (a frivolous practice not unknown in choirs) and would make play on certain words. In Psalm 102, when we reached the words 'I have

[3] There is the story of a canon – and ardent cricketer – who, when visiting a cathedral, would scan the nave and wonder if it would take spin.

watched, and am even as it were a sparrow that sitteth alone upon the housetops', he would look upwards and wipe his eye. The same man provided further 'entertainment' whenever Greene's anthem *Lord, let me know mine end* was being sung. The concluding bars of 'before I go hence and be no more seen' was the signal for heads to turn in his direction to see him lowering himself gradually in his stall until he had disappeared from sight. I have witnessed incredible happenings in many churches, and while irreverence is much to be deplored, it would seem that any amusing diversion, particularly when unintentional, will always raise a smile, even in the most exalted places. I recall a rather shocking incident which occurred over fifty years ago, and disrupted a cathedral service. It concerned the very eccentric (to say the least!) wife of a bishop. She was a dear lady of large proportions, well-liked and given to good works, and for whom much sympathy was felt. But she was prone to break wind, much to the embarrassment of her family and friends. This unfortunate affliction, of which she seemed to be entirely unaware, whenever or wherever it occurred, was said to be caused by her obsessive craving for artichokes, one of the most anti-social of vegetables. She was known to consume them in large quantities, with disastrous repercussions. (As a very devout lady she may have had a preference for Jerusalem artichokes.) All efforts to restrain her had failed, even to the extent of the gardener being instructed to cease growing them. But her *tour-de-force* (!) occurred during an Evensong. She was seated in the stalls behind the choir, when the somnolence induced by the drone of the First Lesson was rudely shattered as she broke wind with startling ferocity! Choirboys tittered, lay clerks choked, and there were discreet coughs amid a flutter of handkerchiefs in the congregation, while clergy had their heads bowed low. Never did a Magnificat have such a shaky start, despite efforts by the organist to hold it together!

In 1945, Sheffield Exham, Vicar of Richmond, Yorkshire, was installed as Canon and Precentor. He came to Lichfield with a high reputation for his intoning. A former minor canon at Windsor and priest vicar of York Minster, he was held in high respect by Sir Walford Davies, who saw to it that Exham was often heard in broadcast services. His fine voice not infrequently added an extra bass part in the choir.

Exham was meticulous as a master of ceremonies and would never allow an ordinary everyday procession to go unrehearsed. To ensure uniformity of movement he would chalk crosses (of no doctrinal significance!) at the turning points in the aisles of the cathedral, on which every boy and man was instructed to pivot. Nautical rolls were unappreciated. We were told to take short steps and to keep our heads still. While these instructions may not have been received with unanimous approval by the choir, it must be admitted that, overall, it was most effective. But it was not easy at the same time to concentrate on singing.

Amusing happenings can occur during processions. Once, when I was a boy, a large pile of chewed gum somehow fell from an unknown source during a procession. We all ploughed on through a kind of Wrigley's quagmire, and as each lad passed through, so his feet became entangled in a sort of elastic skein as the stuff stretched seemingly endlessly. At Lichfield there was a tense incident when two lay vicars stopped singing during a procession to indulge in a loud argument, each accusing the other of not singing during certain verses of the hymn.

The posture of the singing man during services has long been a target for clergy and organists, and not without justification. At Lichfield and elsewhere I have seen men lean, sag, bend, arms folded, arms akimbo, chins cupped in hands, and hands up to ears, and legs crossed. Gordon Reynolds, in his hilarious book *Organo Pleno* (which he did me the honour of dedicating to me), had the following to say about the posture of singers, under the heading of 'Lay Clerks':

> There are many theories about the origin of this term for cathedral choirmen. The title may bear some relation to the traditional posture of the appellant. It may refer to the one factor common to all his actions in the choir stalls — a sense of reclining, which no doubt induces a feeling of relaxation. The use of the archaic term 'lay' instead of 'lie' has caused confusion. There is no evidence that it could refer to ovulation. Records reveal no instance of any lay clerks, not even an alto, actually laying anything.

The following story was told by a former Windsor Chapter Clerk. A young lady (!) answered an advertisement for an alto lay clerk at St George's Chapel. She said she could sing alto and was an expert shorthand typist. But she was not quite sure what the term 'lay' meant!

One lay clerk I knew always sang a solo with his forefinger held pensively under his chin. He said it helped concentration. Another stood on tiptoe when reaching for high notes, while yet another dropped his chin on to his chest when descending to low notes. Yet curiously enough all these men were established professional singers, who adopted a perfectly correct posture on the concert platform. I have known lay clerks who have claimed to be less nervous on a concert platform than in the choir stalls of a cathedral.

In 1950 the first alto vacancy for more than 20 years occurred at St George's Chapel, Windsor Castle. I had known Drs W H Harris and E H Fellowes for some years, and they had both indicated from time to time that they would like me to go to Windsor. But I was so well established at Lichfield, as well as in the midlands and north generally, that it needed some serious heart-searching as to whether I could make the change. It would mean giving up my freehold and deserting a host of friends and colleagues. I had further misgivings about living in the damp and enervating Thames Valley climate – the 'singer's grave', as has been said – which seemingly had bad effects on previous generations of Windsor singers. However, I had found the Trent Valley conducive to colds and catarrh, and in that sense only within Belloc's abuse as 'sodden and unkind'. When I asked Dr Harris about the matter he quoted a profound observation of Dean Baillie that the Windsor climate was 'alright to those it suits'. My wife and sons, however, were in favour of the move, and the attractions of St George's and its world-famed musical traditions, together with a free house in the Castle, finally prevailed. My place at Lichfield was taken by Raymond Leang, a fine alto from St George's Church, Stockport, where the renowned organist Dr Harold Dawber maintained a high musical tradition.

CHAPTER SEVEN

St George's Chapel in Windsor Castle

The house in the 15th-century Horseshoe Cloisters in Windsor Castle which I was to occupy was part of the traditional house of the organist, and had been occupied by a long list of illustrious musicians which included Sir George Elvey, Sir Walter Parratt and, latterly, Sir William Harris. At the time of my appointment, when there was no suitable house vacant for me, Sir William suggested that his house, which he had long considered too big and rambling, should be converted, and a self-contained portion made available for me. Lord Mottistone, the Castle architect, was consulted about necessary structural alterations, and the result was a most attractive house of tremendous character overlooking the west front of the Chapel and Cloister lawn. The sitting room had a magnificent window of leaded glass, and an upstairs window at the back commanded views of the Thames over to Taplow, with the Marlow hills in the distance.

A century ago the kitchen was used as a practice room for the choirboys by Sir George Elvey. The entrance to the house is in the little cloister dwarfed by the huge Curfew Tower which houses the bells of the Chapel. I never quite got used to the sound of the eight bells of the Chapel. They chime every three hours and play the tunes 'St David's' and 'The King's Change'. The clock mechanism dates back to 1689, and was an ingenious device by John Davies. For years I lay in bed in the early hours waiting for those chimes.

So much has been written of the history and glories of St George's Chapel that anything I could hope to add would be superfluous. I found it quite enchanting from the start, and not least the forest of carved 15th-century choir stalls, with their imagery and stories, described by M R James as being 'unrivalled in this country for richness and delicacy'. The eye is drawn upwards to the colourful banners and helmets and swords, which make a dramatic sight. The stall plates – of which there are about 700 – of the Knights of the Garter are world-famous, and represent Knights from the 14th century to the present day. They gleam enchantingly in the rays of the sun, or in the diffused light of the rows of electric candles.

To step into St George's is to leave the world behind. Time is suspended in the sheer beauty all around, and you might well be in the company of Samuel Pepys, who visited the Chapel on 26th February, 1666, and wrote as follows:

> So took coach to Windsor and thither sent for Dr Childe, who came to us and carried us to St. George's Chappell, and there placed us among the Knights' stalls (and pretty the observation, that no man, but a woman, may sit in a Knight's place, where any brass plates are set); and hither come cushions to us, and a young singing-boy to bring us a copy of the anthem to be sung. And here, for our sakes, had this anthem and the great service sung extraordinary, only to entertain us. It is a noble place indeed, and a good choir of voices.

It was in this setting that I found myself, and I was well received with my family by all members of the Chapel, or College as it is known. The Dean, Bishop Eric Hamilton, I had known when he was Bishop of Shrewsbury, and I never saw a more dignified nor hansomer dean. An aristocrat, rather retiring but easy to talk to, he looked the part to Trollopian perfection. He earned for himself the name of the 'Blue Dean', for his Conservative leanings presumably, and in contra-distinction to Hewlett Johnson, the 'Red Dean' of Canterbury. He was a master of diplomacy, which he evinced on many occasions, and on one particular instance which I witnessed. During the sermon one Sunday morning the wrath of a minor canon was aroused as the preacher criticised Anglo-Catholics, whom he described as 'those church folk who imitate Roman Catholicism, and think they are the quintessance of holiness'. The minor canon (an Anglo-Catholic) rose to his feet and exploded 'Nonsense, he's no right to talk like that' (he'd forgotten to switch off his microphone!) After the service he complained to the Dean, who replied: 'Oh, what did he say, I didn't hear it, I was asleep!' He could also be outspoken, and he once pre-faced his sermon to the congregation thus: 'I have received complaints of long sermons, but no one ever complains about short ones. In this funny community (!) I find people taking out their watches to time sermons, and please don't do it.' After which admonition the con-gregation raised their eyebrows, and settled down to doze.

Of the 'characters' who were regular attenders at St George's ser-vices, none was more colourful than Mrs Ford, widow of Dr Lionel

Ford, a former Dean of York, and daughter of a former Bishop of Winchester. She was tall, gaunt and aristocratic, and had a deep, booming voice. She had a house in the Cloisters, and her son, Sir Edward Ford, was Assistant Private Secretary to the Queen. She became a regular visitor to our house, and was friendly with my wife. She had fascinating reminiscences of the great and famous, and she told us of her experience of being the last person to see Cosmo Gordon Lang, the retired Archbishop of Canterbury, before he died suddenly in 1945. As Lord Lang of Lambeth, he was living in Kew, and Mrs Ford had been staying at his house. Before saying goodbye he took her into his little chapel to give her his blessing, after which he had to hurry off to an appointment, and on the way to the station he collapsed and died.

Mrs Ford had great charm, infectious gaiety, and a real sense of humour. In St George's she would join loudly in the monotoned parts of the service – in particular the Creed – an octave lower than the note pitched by the minor canon (round about a bottom A or G in the bass stave), and not even Dr Harris could do anything about that. She often wore a fox fur, which she had the habit of swinging. At the end of one service she stood up and gave it a mighty swing, and caught my son John, who had been sitting next to her, a terrific swipe in the eye. She went off completely unaware of what had happened.

The three residentiary canons were Malcolm Venables, Duncan Armytage, and the colourful Alec Vidler, later Dean of King's College, Cambridge. To see Vidler sweeping through the Cloisters in his red corduroy trousers, black shirt and white tie could never be forgotten. His sermons were dynamic, and he would commence with remarks like this: 'I am going to talk to the choirboys this morning: the rest of the congregation may go to sleep.' He would then enter into a question-and-answer session with the boys. He conducted a most successful seminary in his Cloisters' house for older ordinands, who became known as 'Vidler's Doves'.

St George's has always been noted for the distinction of its minor canons, who when I arrived were Edmund H Fellowes, Christopher Hare and Aubrey Pike. I was glad to renew my acquaintance with Dr Fellowes, who had been a minor canon for 50 years; his impeccable intoning is an abiding memory. During the whole of his time at Windsor he lived in the 15th-century house in Denton's Commons known as 'Marbecke's'. John Marbecke, whose *The Boke of Common Praier Noted* appeared in 1550, and who narrowly escaped being burnt at the stake for his extreme views against Romanism, also lived here, 'singing merrily and playing on the organs'. This remarkably fine house is now occupied by the organist, and the room with a minstrels' gallery is used as a song school. One evening, as I passed this house, I saw Dr Fellowes through a leaded window, writing by candlelight. It was an unforgettable picture as he leaned forward with his spectacles on the end of his rather acquiline nose. He scorned electric light and other modern amenities.

He died in December, 1951, at the age of 81. As Dean Hamilton said of him: 'he did not suffer fools gladly'. He was a law unto himself, which nobody challenged. I remember an occasion when the choir was lined up in the aisle for Evensong, and the Dean and all the canons were absent. 'No canons?' he said, 'then there will be no service' – and there wasn't! (Another choral Evensong was cancelled at a moment's notice by Dr Harris when he discovered that all the choirboys had gone to the pictures with the Dean, after he had given them a party, and the organist had not been informed).

The verger was Fred Buike, MVO, an ex-naval man, in whom Princess Elizabeth and Princess Margaret took an interest during the time they spent in Windsor Castle during the war. He had great dignity and was a real presence. Wilfred Hake, a sacristan succeeded him, and it was often jokingly observed that St George's had on its staff a Hare, a Pike, and a Hake!

Organists of St George's who have left their mark on church music include John Marbecke, Richard Farrant and John Mundy, all of whom flourished in the 16th century; William Child (1632–97), George J Elvey (1835–82), Walter Parratt (1882–1924), Walford Davies (1927–31), Hylton Stewart (1932–33), William H Harris (1933–61) and Sidney Campbell (1961–74).

I sang under Dr Harris (later Sir William) from 1951 until his retirement in 1961. He was formerly assistant organist at Lichfield, and organist of Christ Church and New College, Oxford. He gave music lessons to the Queen and Princess Margaret when they were children, and he formed a madrigal group in which they took part. A product of the Parratt school at Windsor, he was usually referred to as 'Doc H'. He maintained a rigid discipline with his choir, and drove himself as hard as he drove his singers. He was fastidious to a degree, and was completely dedicated to his work. No slackness was tolerated, full attendance was demanded, and he was rarely absent. On one occasion he fell from a stage while he was conducting a choir at Eton. Although he injured his head and was badly shocked, he was back on duty in the organ loft next day.

The only time I had any time off from choir was when I had to spend several weeks in hospital, following an accident which fractured my pelvis. The day I was discharged from hospital and back at home in the Cloisters, I had a visit from Doc H. I was still on crutches and feeling rather weak. After welcoming me warmly, he said: 'While there is no immediate hurry for you to return to the choir, I wouldn't delay it too long, as you will feel much better for being in action again.' I hobbled into Evensong next day, and listened to the singing from the nave, and it affected me to the extent that the very next morning, in spite of vigorous protests from my wife, sons and colleagues, I seized my crutches and made my way slowly to the Chapel. The boys were practising as I passed the Song School, and they all came rushing out to greet me. Doc H, beaming, said: 'There's Mr Hodgson, and I know where he is going. Use him as an example boys, and give him a cheer.' With those cheers ringing in my ears, I went to the vestry and put on my cassock and surplice, went into Chapel, and sat in my stall, and waited for the choir to process in. At Evensong that day the anthem was appropriately Goss's *The Wilderness*, and I sang in the trio − 'Strengthen ye the weak hands, and confirm the feeble knees'. As I balanced on my crutches I was certainly given strength (I needed it), and I felt better for the experience, which made me appreciate that Doc H knew me better than I realised. I recovered rapidly, and was soon able to run about again.

There were many tense early-morning practices with Doc H, often in critical mood, and everyone had to be on his toes. On occasion an aggrieved lay clerk would retaliate, with the inevitable 'fireworks'. But Doc H had a sense of humour, and once when he said to the choir: 'You are turning out every note like sausages from a machine', a voice from somewhere queried: 'Harris's?' He appreciated that and joined in the laughter, and peace was restored. He maintained and upheld the Parratt tradition of an inhibited, impersonal style of singing in which any form of individuality was anathema. After leaving behind the far less inhibited singing at Lichfield, this apparent repression was something I had to get used to. His subordinate position is a condition any dedicated lay clerk accepts, with an inevitable conformity to any contemporary cult, fashion or school influencing choral trends. A term seldom heard nowadays is that of the 'cathedral voice', which referred to a particularly fine voluminous sound, suited to vast spaces, and effective equally in solo or ensemble. That there is a comparative scarcity of such voices cannot be denied. But a fundamental cause, and one which tends to be overlooked, is that while there is no reason to believe that there has been physiological degeneration in the human voice, there have, however, been radical changes in the methods of using it, particularly in choral singing, which are only too apparent to those with a lifetime's experience of choirs.

Choral activity in this country was at its peak in the last quarter of the 19th century, and it produced definite trends and divergent schools, ranging from an inhibited bloodless style of chamber singing associated with certain of the smaller academic choirs, to the robust dynamic singing of the 'big battalion' church choirs, particularly in the north, which was often demanded by unresonant buildings (it is well known what flattering acoustics can do).

The appointment of Walter Parratt to St George's, Windsor, in 1882, set a trend in an impersonal style of singing which I have previously mentioned and which influenced choirs mainly in academic circles for many years. E H Fellowes, in *Organists and Masters of the Choristers of St George's Chapel, Windsor Castle*, says of Parratt: 'As an interpreter of Church Music, some of his critics saw, perhaps with good reason, that at times his inherent classicism led to undue coldness of expression.' Sir William Harris, in his Presidential Address to the Royal College of Organists in July 1947, also says of Parratt:

His ideals of singing were no doubt coloured by the impersonal style of his organ-playing. I am told he would have such anthems as *Lord, for Thy tender mercies sake*, sung without nuance or variation of tone colour whatever in a perfectly level unimpassive style. That he succeeded in making his choir sing in this impersonal style (under much protest I am told) is remarkable, seeing that he had some very fine solo voices among his lay clerks.

It need hardly be said that voices of marked individuality have always presented a problem in ensemble singing; yet conversely it should be remembered that small, undistinguished voices can only be expected to produce indifferent sounds. The technique applied may be excellent, and by their very nature they may be more likely to 'blend'. But it is

just as illogical to assume that any great range of dynamics or grada-
tion of tone colour can be achieved by such voices, as it is to assert
that fine solo voices cannot be disciplined and balanced into a perfectly
satisfactory blend. Of the solo voice in choirs, Harvey Grace in his
Choral Conducting says:

> When they can be persuaded to blend they cease to be danger-spots, and
> become towers of strength. Singers with good tone may give a bad per-
> formance, but those with bad tone cannot really give a good one.

The renaissance of polyphonic music during the 20th century has led
to a radical approach to, and a new conception of, tone in English
choral singing. This has evolved from a doctrine propagated by
musicologists and those influenced by Continental habits, together
with protagonists of the neo-baroque organ school, with its predilection for inducing a sharp, edgy tonal structure which claims greater
clarity and definition that can be achieved, it is imagined, by the
strictly round full voice, which may be thought to be too thick in
registration and so loaded with overtones for anything but homophonic
effects, and anachronistic in music other than that of such composers
as Stanford and Charles Wood, suggesting 'Anglican neo-Gothic,
rather than Rossini clarity'.

Further attempts have been made to try and justify the white, open
edgy sound as being 'authentic' to music of the Renaissance and
Baroque periods. But how can such claims be anything but conjec-
ture? Charles Kennedy Scott, in 'Points for Madrigal Singers', in his
Euterpe series, says: 'Linear clearness can be achieved as a rule only
by using "open" tone: tone in which reedy nasal resonance has full
play'.

The article on 'Baroque interpretation' in *Grove V*, by Robert
Donington, makes these points: 'For polyphonic music, the quality
of voice which singers refer to as "white" is of general service ...
Brightness in early polyphony is best secured by a nasal twang, similar
in kind, though not in degree, to that characteristic of so many
Oriental styles ... Bel Canto and florid singing should not be white
at all, but the reasons for the decline in these exacting arts seem
unknown, even to the experts.' This raises the question: who are the
experts?

These classical misconceptions of vocal tone completely negate the
very foundations on which our best English choral traditions were

built, by which, through emphasis on sheer beauty of tone and variety of tone colour and crispness of enunciation, any degree of linear definition can be attained.

My lay clerk colleagues at St George's were all greatly experienced singers, with a remarkably high standard of musicianship. The senior lay clerk, Fred Naylor, was one for whom I had a great affection and regard. He came to Windsor from Peterborough Cathedral in 1895, and retired from St George's in 1957 at the age of 84. He was the last of the freehold, or life tenure, lay clerks, and he had been renowned for the beauty of his alto voice. He sang at the Diamond Jubilee celebrations of Queen Victoria in 1897, and at her funeral, and also at the funerals of Edward VII, George V, and George VI. He had the distinction of singing at four Coronations. We sang together on the decani side, and soon became firm friends. He was the best type of dedicated lay clerk, gentlemanly, refined, and always immaculately dressed. He died in 1963 at the age of 91.

My other alto colleagues were Wallis Searle and Cyril Simkins, both formerly of Tenbury, making all three of us ex-St Michael's. 'Wally' Searle was a fine choral singer, and he was noted for his fund of funny stories and reminiscences. He and I would often swap our respective collections, and he would be telling a story or anecdote as we started to process through the Cloisters, and as we arrived at the Chapel door, he would say: 'and on that note, gentlemen, the levity must now cease. We will now enter Divine Service.' He was fond of relating how, after singing glees to King George V, the King had said: 'Now why don't you sing like that in Chapel?'

Cyril Simkins, known to everyone as 'Simmie', was another distinctive character. A Devonian, he had come to St George's via Tenbury and Gloucester, and became well known for his editing of church music ranging from the Middle Ages to the Restoration.[1] He was a particularly fine penman, and compiled notable chant books, written out beautifully, and specially commissioned by several cathedrals, and also at St George's and Westminster Abbey, where they were used daily for many years. He had a mane of white hair, and a ruddy

---

[1] Simkins collaborated with E H Fellowes in an edition of Purcell's *Bell Anthem (Rejoice in the Lord)*, undertaken 'at the unanimous request of the Cathedral Organists' Association in Session, November 1950'. Other editions were of Blow's *My God, My God* (Chester 1953), Robert Stone's *The Lord's Praier* (SPCK 1934), the *Windsor Series of Polyphonic Music* (Hinrichsen), and a *University Carol Book* (Freeman).

countenance, which grew ruddier when he was upset. He made his presence felt in more ways than one, and was outspoken. He would air a grievance usually connected with clergy or organists in no uncertain terms. As one who stood next to him in the choir for many years, I became used to his asides, and his stage whispered observations – which were often devastatingly humorous – during service.

Doc H was (rightly) of the opinion that conducting in church should never be ostentatious, nor too vigorous, and he made only the minimum amount of movement with his hands. At Evensong one day, as he was conducting the anthem, 'Simmie', in impish mood, nudged me and said: 'Look, Freddy, he's brought his knitting.' I have heard the conducting of some organists as being like 'pulling a chain', 'cleaning a window', or 'doing a bit of dusting'. I sometimes wonder if nowadays church choirs are being over-conducted? This may be a controversial point, but is it really necessary for almost every word of Responses, Psalms and Amens, to say nothing of the monotoned parts of the service, to be conducted? Years ago, when there was much less conducting in choirs, unanimity could be achieved by establishing a rapport with, and keeping a strict eye on, one's counterpart on the other side, even to the extent of breathing together. Ambrose Porter of Lichfield, believed that a good, well-disciplined choir needed only the minimum amount of conducting, and Conrad Eden, organist of Durham Cathedral (1936–1974), said that: 'The ensemble a good choir develops was sufficient to keep choir and organ together.' He refused to have a mirror in the organ loft, and would keep the curtains closed. During the rebuilding of the organ in 1969, he vigorously rejected the suggestion that closed-circuit television should be included.

At a service when the basses had been laid low by illness, Doc H came down into the choir, and asked 'Simmie' to forsake the alto line and sing bass with him, and their combined efforts were very accurate if unusual. As we sat down for the lesson 'Simmie' turned to me and said: 'How did you like our wheelbarrow tone?' He would refer to some singers as producing a 'bass-broom' quality, or 'letter-box' tone. He was himself a countertenor with an extended lower register. I missed him very much after he retired in 1967.

The tenors when I arrived were Albert Key, Bamfield (Archie) Cooper, and Tom Pinder. Albert Key was a musicianly singer, and a former lay clerk of St John's College, Cambridge. Archie Cooper, a Bristolian, won a scholarship to the Royal College of Music, and later went into opera at Covent Garden. The possessor of a robust voice of splendid quality, he was appointed to St George's on the recommendation of Sir Hugh Allen. Tom Pinder, a Yorkshireman from Halifax, was a keen young lyric tenor, well known for his dedication to church music. He made a specialised study of plainsong and also did notable work in an executive capacity over many years for the Guild of Church Musicians.

The basses were Robert Davies, Arthur Raine and Cyril Ash. Robert Davies was a former RCM student and a protege of Sir Walford Davies. A Welshman from Wrexham, he had an excellent baritone voice, and became a well known broadcaster. He taught singing at Eton College for many years.

Arthur Raine was another Yorkshireman, with a delicious accent, who came from York Minster. As well as being an accomplished singer he was also something of a humorist. He had to take care of his health, and was particularly susceptible to draughts. During service in the nave one bitterly cold morning, he sang with his surplice pulled up over his head like a hood, and when he saw that someone had left the door open it was more than he could stand, and he shouted to a colleague opposite 'go and shut t'door!' Once, during a Communion Service, a choirboy was sick all over his stall. Arthur was horrified, and he immediately left the stalls to disappear rapidly through the choir screen. He reappeared a moment or two later swinging a bucket of sand, which he poured unceremoniously over the mess on the stall as the singing went on, that is, insofar as it could have been said to have gone on in such a situation. Amid a minor tumult in the congregation we tried to pull ourselves together when Doc H looked down from the organ loft, and said: 'What's going on down there?' What was going on soon became apparent to him.

Cyril Ash had one of those rare foundation bass voices which are an asset to any choir. As senior lay clerk he was much concerned about the welfare of his colleagues, whom he represented so excellently and effectively in his liaison with the Dean and canons.

Congregational singing in parish churches has always been an integral and laudable tradition, and long may congregations enjoy their singing. But in those places where there is a professional choir, singing by members of the congregation is not encouraged, except in hymns. There are always those who insist on joining in, often very much out of tune; or they will have a go at putting in their own harmonies in chants, or singing the monotoned parts of the service on a discordant note, and on occasion even trying to sing in the most complex anthems and services of which they make it quite clear they have no knowledge. Such people readily assert that a church is a place of worship, and that anyone therefore should be allowed to lift up his voice in praise. But it is usually those least fitted vocally who can ruin a cathedral service. A famous story of Dr Varley Roberts, a forthright Yorkshireman if there ever was one, who was organist of Magdalen Colege, Oxford, is worth repeating. A visitor to a service (said to be a bishop) joined in the singing lustily, which infuriated the doctor, who dashed down the organ loft steps after service and chased the man and ticked him off roundly. 'But', replied the offender on an injured tone, 'I thought one was allowed to lift up one's voice in the House of God?' 'No', said the doctor, 'I would remind you that this is not the House of God, it's Magdalen College Chapel.'

Doc H would certainly not tolerate such uninvited 'assistance' from anyone sitting in the congregation, which had its amusing and embarrassing moments. On one occasion, as he heard an offender joining in raucously, his head appeared over the organ loft, and he hissed: 'Who is it?' This caused heads to look upwards, and as he looked down he said very pointedly: 'Don't sing!' This apparently had the desired effect, as the culprit got the message. At one time, another deterrent, printed in red, appeared on the service lists, which read something like this: 'We have inherited a great musical tradition, and members of the congregation are invited to join in the service silently, except in hymns.' Someone in high office objected to this, and the words disappeared from the lists.

Years ago there was a canon who objected to members of the congregation remaining seated throughout the service. These were mostly foreigners unfamiliar with the Anglican service who obviously preferred to observe rather than stand at those points decreed by the established form of service. The canon would tolerate their non-conforming for a while, then he would startle the congregation by calling out loudly: 'Stand up!' I have also seen offenders brought to their feet by an upward tilt of the head from a verger. Churches today are generally more tolerant, taking the view that all visitors are welcome as long as their presence in no way disturbs the service. It is, perhaps, worth making the point that those who visit our ancient and beautiful churches and cathedrals can only really begin to know them when they can in some way appreciate their purpose and function. One sees hordes of tourists every summer scurrying out of every cathedral in the land when Evensong is about to commence.

CHAPTER EIGHT
State occasions

I *The funeral of King George VI (15th February 1952)*

I did not sleep well the night before the funeral. I kept waking up, to catch a glint of light coming through the great west window of the Chapel. The film cameras had been installed in our front bedroom, and in the semi-darkness they made fantastic shapes. The day started with a calling-up from Fred Buike next door. The cameramen were at the house by 8 o'clock, in time for a communal breakfast that had been designed with characteristic Yorkshire skill and generosity by my wife. The windows then were taken out of the front bedroom and the stage was now almost ready for the great drama.

During the morning there was one tiresome incident when a pompous and officious colonel, in busby, told us and our colleagues and guests that no one was allowed to stand outside on our verandas. *'They must all be indoors'*, he barked. At this there was all but a riot, as lay clerks and their families and friends from time immemorial had enjoyed the right to watch all state ceremonies from their verandas. Fred Buike, the verger, and some of the lay clerks stood on their rights, and told the functionary that the houses in the Cloisters were our homes (with the implication that they were, therefore, also 'castles') and that neither our families nor guests had any intention of moving. The order was rescinded. We were able to rope off our fronts and we duly put out rows of chairs.

The Archbishops took part in a short rehearsal, and, towards noon, the atmosphere became more tense, with an air of expectancy. The Grenadier Guards marched onto the Cloister lawn and took up their positions. By early afternoon it was estimated that somewhere in the region of 100,000 people were in Windsor. My family and guests seated themselves on the veranda and I went into the Chapel, passing through crowds of mourners and countless wreaths from all manner of people, and from children too. We robed and assembled in the choir aisle.

The moment had arrived. We processed slowly to the bottom of the nave, with Hake and Warner, the sacristans, leading. We stood facing inwards, with our heels touching the edge of the blue carpet. We were at that moment the centre of all eyes, and as one cast around a discreet glance it was a truly amazing congregation that surrounded us. People of many lands – most of them famous in their day – were seated in the tiers built in the nave aisles.

Fred Buike led the Archbishops to the open West Door to await the funeral procession. There was a hush. The sun shone. The great crosses of Canterbury and York glinted. And there was a two-minute silence. Then, in the words of George Murray: *'The outside world penetrated the peace and sanctuary ... distant orders and the faint click of arms ... hoof beats ... heart beats, nearer it came ... bosun's pipes, and we knew the King had been piped overboard.'*

We turned and processed up the nave singing Croft's *Burial Sentences*: 'I am the resurrection and the life'. I was relieved when this moment arrived as we were beginning to feel the strain of waiting. As we passed under the organ screen we brushed by the Yeomen of the Guard and the Military Knights, and so into the brilliance of the choir, where the stalls were filled with illustrious figures from all over the world.

We took up our places in the Sanctuary, and I found myself standing behind a huge candlestick, though I had a good view of the ceremony. A dramatic moment was when the coffin slowly descended from our sight. The young Queen stepped forward and sprinkled earth into the grave ... 'Ashes to ashes ...'. The singing of *God be in my head*, by Sir Walford Davies, a former organist of St George's, brought the service to a fitting close. We filed passed the open grave and looked down on the coffin draped in the Royal Standard, and the single wreath inscribed with the name 'Elizabeth'.

My family had thrilling accounts of all they had seen, and were particularly impressed with the sailors pulling the gun-carriage. From early morning the next day there was an influx of 200,000 visitors to Windsor, and at one point there was a three-mile queue to see the wreaths. What a struggle it was to enter or leave the Castle! I had been issued with a resident's pass, but I had to be 'rescued' by police before the crowd would let me through.

At St George's a colourful feature is provided by the Military Knights, who represent the Knights of the Garter on Sunday morning.

They are high-ranking army officers of some distinction in their profession and live in Lower Ward of the Castle under their Governor, who in my time was General Sir Edmund Hakewill-Smith. In Chapel they wear brilliant scarlet uniforms. When a new Knight is installed, or at the Presentation at the Altar of the banner of a departed Knight of the Garter, there is a click of heels, the obeisance to the Sovereign's Stall, and the heavy cadential tread, all performed with a strong sense of theatre.

There were inevitably characters among them, and none more than my namesake, Colonel Christopher Hodgson. As my younger son is named Christopher, and a keen fisherman, the old Colonel – also an angler – took to him, and we often visited his house. Conversations usually centred on angling, and he loved to tell the tale of how he fell into the lake at Frogmore when trying to land a huge pike. There would be a constant striking of matches as he tried to light his pipe, and he would throw the spent matches on to an expensive carpet, while his wife bobbed round protestingly as she picked them up. He had two dogs respectively named 'Blimey' and 'Tinker'. 'Blimey' had a hideously misshapen mouth which was caused by getting in the way of one of the Colonel's golf balls. Colonel Hodgson was in his eighties when he died, and the last time I saw him I hailed as usual with 'Good morning, Colonel, how are you?' 'Bloody old', he muttered as he shuffled by without looking up.

Another peppery brigadier had an obsession about loud organ playing, and once as a voluntary ended with some quite shattering chords, he spluttered loudly: 'I thought this was a consecrated building!' This same brigadier also objected to foreign cars, and I saw him wave his stick and shout 'Hun' as one sped past through the Castle gate.

The Military Knights represent to the world at large the embodiment of the idea of 'fine old English gentlemen', so one may notice how they courteously doff their hats as they acknowledge the salute of a sentry. Most of them are immaculate in dress, and for all occasions. They are to be seen in their toppers heading for Ascot or a garden party at Buckingham Palace, or in their bowlers when they are rehearsing for a Garter Procession, which is always led by the Military Knights.

The author - age 12.

The author - drawing by E Keyte, 1945.

The Rev Sir
Frederic A Gore
Ouseley and (left) St
Michael's College,
Tenbury (drawing by
Chris Hodgson).

Sheffield Cathedral (drawing by Chris Hodgson).

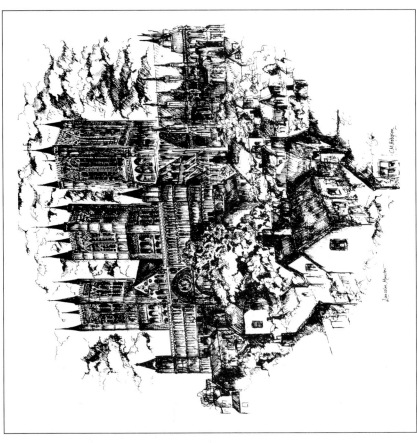

Dr George Bennett in 1929 and (right) Lincoln Cathedral (drawing by Chris Hodgson).

Lichfield Cathedral

Above: The author and his son John when members of the Lichfield Cathedral choir.
Below: The author's son Christopher as a chorister at Eton College, 1954. He was later to provide several of the drawings for this book.

Right: Ambrose Porter.

HM The Queen chatting to Lichfield Cathedral choirboys in 1946. Fourth from left is the author's son, John.

Right: Presentation to Sir William Harris on his retirement in 1961. Front row: Dr Gerald Knight, Sir William Harris, Clement McWilliam. Back row: Tom Pinder, Robert Davies, Bamfield Cooper, Philip Howell, Frederic Hodgson, Cyril Ash and Arthur Raine.

Part of Horseshoe Cloister, St George's, Windsor (photo by Alan Kendall).

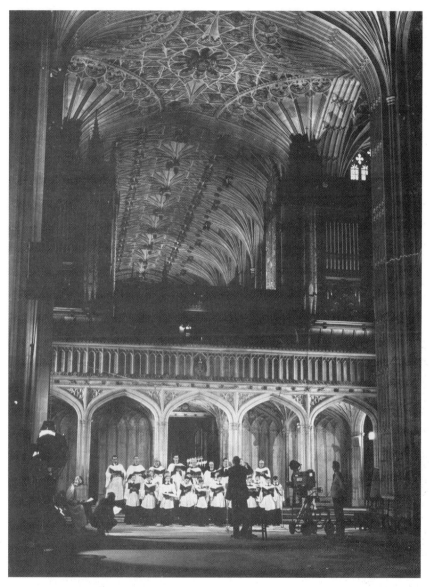

Christmas music being recorded in the Queen's Free Chapel of St George,
Windsor, on Christmas Eve 1962. Conducting is Dr Sidney Campbell.

Above: Malcolm Boyle with Sir
John Barbirolli (*centre*) and Mrs
Boyle.

The author's wife, Beth (1959).

Above: 'Chuck' Hodgson (photo by Brian Pratt)

Below: Dr Sidney Campbell in 1973 with Andrew Whitehouse, Patrick Whitby, Gavin Purssel and Colin Nicholson.

Above: (left to right): Stanley
Riley, Frederic Hodgson,
Alfred Hepworth and
Kenneth Tudor (photo by
Alfred Hepworth).

Right: Frederic Hodgson as a
Gentleman of the Chapel
Royal in 1977 (photo by
Alfred Hepworth).

Sir William Harris (from a painting by Michael Brockway, 1957).

The Rev Dr Edmund H Fellowes.

The Chapel Royal at St James's (drawing by Chris Hodgson), *copyright reserved.*

The Chapel Royal Choir in 1977. Back row: Graham Trew, John Watts, Matthew Graham, Colin Scull, John Lake, Richard Lewis. Second row: Mark Thomas, Neil Thomas, Bruce Trathen, Gavin Kibble, Michael Cave, Colin Campbell. Third row: Frederic Hodgson, Norman Cooper, Timothy Farrell, Canon James Mansel, Peter Goldspink, Richard Edwards. Front row: Giles Stockton, John Coutts, Robert Sawdy, Michael Hughes.

The choirs of St Paul's Cathedral and the Chapel Royal at the Queen's Silver Jubilee Thanksgiving Service at St Paul's Cathedral in 1977 (photograph by Geoffrey Shaw).

1 Barry Rose (Master of Choristers)
2 Peter Hall
3 Keith Abbs
4 Michael Blackley
5 Simon Hill
6 John Dexter
7 Derek Sutton (Headmaster)
8 Andrew Giles

10 Cyril Taylor
11 Graham Sorrell
12 Roger Heath
13 David Roy
14 Ian Thompson
15 Jonathan Alder
16 Maurice Bevan
17 Owen Grundy
18 Andrew Pearmain
19 Alan Green
20 Christopher Dearnley

21 Geoffrey Shaw
22 Peter Goldspink
23 Richard Edwards
24 Norman Cooper
25 Freddy Hodgson
26 Richard Lewis
27 Andrew Manktelow
28 David Judges
29 Barry Holden
30 Richard Arnatt
31 Adrian Butterfield

33 Paul Wicks
34 Jonathan Clarke
35 Nicolas Mehta
36 Jeremy Carpenter
37 Andrew Williams
38 Julian Rippon
39 Andrew Truswell
40 David Smith
41 Christopher Walker
42 Mark Withers
43 Mark Thomas

45 Gavin Kibble
46 Neil Thomas
47 Bruce Trathan
48 Michael Hughes
49 Robert Sawdy
50 Giles Stockton
51 John Coutts
52 Richard Cave
53 Robert Eaton
54 Dieter Cooke
55 Jeremy Burrows

57 Brinley Page
58 Matthew Barnes
59 David Riggs
60 Adrian Jones
61 David Fisk
62 Christopher Head
63 Craig McLeish
64 Matthew Vine
65 Paul Phoenix
66 Nicholas Johnson

(Assistant Organist)

II *The Coronation of Queen Elizabeth II at Westminster Abbey (2nd June, 1953)*

The highlight of a singer's career is to sing at a Coronation — a privilege which comes only to a few — and as St George's Choir has a prescriptive right to sing at Coronations, the occasion provided one of the most moving experiences of my life. There were seven preliminary rehearsals in St Margaret's, Westminster (four for the boys only), and three final rehearsals summoned by the Earl Marshal in the Abbey. The Duchess of Norfolk acted as stand-in for the Queen. In all these there were some 400 singers, the nucleus being formed by the choirs of Westminster Abbey, the Chapel Royal, St George's, Windsor, and St Paul's Cathedral. There were representatives from the Chapels Royal at Hampton Court and the Tower of London and the Queen's Chapel of the Savoy; Canterbury Cathedral, York Minster, Southwark Cathedral, Llandaff Cathedral, St Mary's Cathedral, Edinburgh, Armagh Cathedral, St Patrick's Cathedral, Dublin, St Anne's Cathedral, Belfast, and Christ Church Cathedral, Oxford; and from Eton College, King's College, Cambridge, the Temple Church, St Margaret's, Westminster, The Royal School of Church Music, All Saints, Margaret Street, Westminster Abbey Special Choir, Westminster Abbey Sunday Evening Choir, as well as representatives from the old dominions. Additional singers included many famous concert artists of the day. There was an orchestra comprising 60 eminent professionals, conducted by Sir Adrian Boult, and the 21 trumpeters were drawn from the Royal Military School, Kneller Hall. There were 15 choir stewards, a doctor and a nurse, and Gerald Knight, Director of the Royal School of Music, acted as Hon Choir Secretary.

After one rehearsal I was with Doctor Harris, talking to Dr Ralph Vaughan Williams, who after commenting on the superb sound of the Coronation Choir, added: 'But where were the *pianissimos*?' He was, however, said to have been delighted with the performance of the music in the service, which included the Credo and the Sanctus from his Mass in G minor, his anthem *O taste and see*, and arrangement of the 'Old Hundredth'. The Director of Music was Dr William McKie, the Abbey Organist, and the sub-conductors were Dr William Harris, of St George's, Windsor, and Dr John Dykes Bower, of St Paul's Cathedral. The organists were Harry Gabb, of the Chapel

Royal, St James's Palace, Henry Ley, late of Eton College, and Dr Osborne Peasgood, sub-organist of Westminster Abbey.

I was up at 4.30 am on Coronation Day, and the choir left Windsor by coach at 5.30. My travelling companion in the coach was Alastair Sampson, a St George's chorister, who at 8 years of age was the youngest singer to take part in the Coronation. He inherited his exceptional musical talents from two famous grandfathers: Sir John Stainer, Organist of St Paul's Cathedral, and Sir Frederick Bridge, Organist of Westminster Abbey. He is now the distinguished Organist at Eton College. It was bitterly cold and wet, but we were warm and snug in the coach. As we drove along, the men chatted animatedly, and the boys found it very difficult not to do the same, even though they had been told to save their voices. The streets, even those leading into the Coronation area, were deserted, and those in Westminster had been cleared for the arrival of the Abbey guests, though there were of course multitudes on the main route waiting patiently. We arrived at the Abbey before 6.30 am, and after robing in the Chapter House we took up our positions in the Cloisters about 7.30. We were standing there, shivering in the cold, and sympathy was felt for the few lady singers from the dominions, whose teeth chattered as they waited in their scanty evening gowns. The delay was due to the procession being held up by the peers and peeresses arriving. We were relieved when we were directed back to wait in the Chapter House.

What a gorgeous sight it was when we finally processed through the 'Theatre': the Abbey plate flashing in the myriad lights, the splendid robes, and the gentle murmur of subdued excitement. We climbed up into our allotted seats on the north side of the orchestra gallery, in the first arch on the Cantoris side of the choir. I was on the end seat of the first row of the altos. The long wait before the processions was full of interest as we spotted one celebrity after another from our vantage point, and listened to the thrilling sounds of the orchestra, conducted by Sir Adrian Boult.

The following directions regarding refreshments had been issued to each member of the choir:

Suitable refreshments may be brought to the robing places on Coronation Day, to be eaten before choir form up for the Procession. If it is desired to take refreshments into the Abbey (to be consumed before or after, *but not during*, the actual service) these should consist of no more than can be carried in the cassock pocket. Sandwiches made with fresh vegetables as well as meat or eggs are recommended, also stoned raisins, and perhaps a small bottle of milk. It is advised that no tea or coffee be taken on the morning of the Coronation.

I had my last cup of tea at 8 o'clock on the previous evening! I had grapes with me, which I slid into my mouth surreptitiously to keep it moist. We were under the impression that once we were in our seats, there could be no leaving them until after the service. But when it got to about 10 o'clock one or two men were getting restless, and a certain lay clerk who had a bladder weakness decided he could not wait any longer, and off he went. As was to be expected, this had a psychological effect on many of us, and soon there was an unofficial procession of men going downstairs. The word 'PEERS' over a loo caused confusion!

Sympathy was felt for the plight of the small boy chorister whose need was urgent. Now a renowned organist, he recalls his discomfiture thus: 'My abiding memory is of the total absence of loos for one hundred or more little boys in a service lasting seven hours! The milk in my one-third pint bottle having gone off by about 12.30, I couldn't drink it, and so had nothing to pee into. Eventually they passed me back like a parcel (the rake was terribly steep and I was terrified), and I toddled to the lay clerks' loo, where the trough was arranged so high I could stand underneath it! Eventually some equally caught-short lay clerk arrived and managed to disentangle me from my robes and dangle me over it. They then passed me back down that steep slope over people's shoulders to my seat in the front row. Heaven only knows what would have happened if there'd been a fire!'

I kept nibbling chicken sandwiches, and chewing chocolate raisins. Several of the men kept having nips from their flasks, leaving a tell-tale whiff more appropriate to the tavern than the Abbey, and some went so far as to smoke during the wait in the Chapter House. There was a bit of a stir and a general titter when, just before the Queen's Procession entered the Abbey, several men and women in white coats rushed through the choir screens, armed with cleaners and sweeping brushes, and began frantically to clean the carpet of any marks left by the previous processions. Not only was the office of 'char' elevated to unprecedented heights, but these were the handmaids of the Lord serving His most exalted servant!

As the processions started, our eyes were glued to the splendid scene: the Queen Mother, smiling as ever, and inclining her head from left to right in regal manner as she scanned the congregation; Princess Margaret, the Royal Duchesses, with their attendant ladies and pages. It was a thrilling moment when the young and lovely Queen came into the Abbey. The fanfares rang out, and the dramatic start of Parry's anthem *I was glad* burst from 400 throats. At this point it was difficult to control one's emotions at the tremendous impact of those opening chords, and the interpolation of the Queen's Scholars of Westminster School with their appropriate traditional shouts: 'Vivat Regina! Vivat Regina! Elizabetha, Vivat, Vivat, Vivat!'. There was a feast of music to follow, with an introit composed for the occasion by Herbert Howells, *Behold, O God, our defender*, and a Gradual, also specially written, by William Harris: *Let my prayer come up*. Then followed the Creed from the Communion Service in G Minor by Vaughan Williams.

During the Anointing the hymn 'Come, Holy Ghost', was sung to an arrangement by Ernest Bullock, who also wrote all the fanfares for the service. Every singer who took part will, I am sure, carry an abiding memory of the singing of Handel's exhilarating *Zadok the Priest*, which was written for the Coronation of George II, and has been sung at every subsequent Coronation. Although I have sung in this anthem so many times, there could be no occasion to match this performance for splendid declamation and precision and build-up in the 'Amen' runs. When the climax of the service was reached — the Putting on of the Crown — I was fortunate to be in a position to see the Archbishop of Canterbury place the Crown upon the Queen's head, and then the Abbey rang with the loud shouts of acclamation: 'God save the Queen!'. Caps and Coronets went on the heads of peers and peeresses, trumpets sounded, and guns were fired from the Tower.

There followed a short anthem, *Be strong* by George Dyson, which preceded five Homage Anthems: *Rejoice in the Lord* (attr. Redford), *O clap your hands* (Orlando Gibbons), *I will not leave you* (Byrd), *O Lord, our Governour* (Healey Willan), and *Thou wilt keep him* (S S Wesley). The hymn which followed, *All people that on earth do dwell*, arranged by Vaughan Williams, with organ and orchestra, and trumpeters playing the descant, provided one of the most moving experiences in the whole service. The Communion Service continued with the *Sanctus* by Vaughan Williams, and then his exquisite short anthem *O taste and see*, written specially for the occasion. In this the greatest admiration was felt for the Abbey boys, who sang the solo part beautifully and nonchalantly. Stanford's great *Gloria* followed, and after the blessing, came the *Threefold Amen* by Gibbons.

In the Preface to the Coronation Music Book, Frank Howes writes as follows of Sir William Walton's *Te Deum*:

> The Te Deum to be sung after the Blessing, specially composed by Sir William Walton, is the most extensive of the new works for this Coronation Service. It is conceived on the most spacious lines for two choirs, two semi-choruses, boys' voices, organ, orchestra and military brass, forces which are deployed for the maximum splendour of effect. The inspiration of this ancient hymn of the Church is inexhaustible, and in this latest most elegant and jubilant setting it provides a worthy climax to a great national occasion of thanksgiving.

The historic ceremony ended brilliantly with Gordon Jacob's setting of the National Anthem, with its fanfares. We were now able to relax and watch the wonderful processions, and what a joy it was to see the newly-crowned Queen carrying her Orb and Sceptre with such composure. I shall never forget the great emotion on the face of Winston Churchill as he processed out of the theatre. He paused under the choir screen and turned and looked back on the scene, and shook his head slightly. We finally got out at 2.30 pm and I found myself mingling with peers and peeresses, several of whom spoke to me of the wonderful singing of the choir. A last look around the glittering Theatre, and so to the Chapter House to disrobe and join in the excited chatter. In the Cloisters, choirboys were crowding round a table laden with refreshments, while their elders were disposing of champagne and sherry.

We returned to Windsor by coach, and when I reached home I was so dehydrated I drank six cups of tea straight off! Later we saw the service on television, the first Coronation to be televised. The only thing which might have spoiled a wonderful occasion was the weather. But nothing, I am sure, could have dampened the ardour and sincerity of all those who shouted: 'God save the Queen!'. Every member of the choir received the Coronation Medal from the Queen.

III *The Funeral of the Duke of Windsor (5th June 1972)*

The death of Edward, Duke of Windsor, at the age of 77, occurred on 20th May, 1972. As Edward VIII he had reigned for only ten months, and after his Abdication in 1936, he wrote, 'It may be some time before I return'; and a sad return it was.

Preparations for royal funerals and those of great national figures are – as far as possible – made well in advance, and are implemented by an official swing into action after a death is announced. As always, the Chapel was prepared for the Duke's lying-in-state, and services were suspended.

My wife's prowess as a needlewoman was well known, and Canon Bentley, the Precentor, asked her if she would shorten a cope to be worn by the Dean at the funeral, as Launcelot Fleming – Dean from 1971 to 1976 – was not so tall as his immediate predecessors. The intricate work took hours to complete. The magnificent cope, previously used at the funeral of King George VI, is black with a patterned gold brocade and black velvet facings.

World attention was again focussed on Windsor, and at one period there was a two-mile queue to see the lying-in-state. I watched the scene as the endless stream passed up the Chapel steps into the nave to file past the catafalque, on which the coffin was draped with the Duke's own personal standard. There were many among the crowds old enough to have remembered the man as a popular symbol of their youth. It was said that 59,000 people witnessed the lying-in-state.

I went into the Chapel at night, long after it had been closed to the public, and I have never seen the nave look so enchanting. There was a dim mellow light from the great candles round the catafalque, and the fan-vaulting – the great glory of the Chapel – was subtly floodlit. The Household Cavalry, with bent heads, keeping their long vigil, looking like statues. The only sound was the sword-tap order of command. Outside, the Dean's Cloister was heavy with the scent of a multitude of wreaths, and among them from the great and famous, was one tiny anonymous posy, inscribed: 'God rest his noble loyal soul; his exile is over'.

On the evening of June 3rd, the Duchess of Windsor was escorted into the Chapel by the Prince of Wales and Earl Mountbatten. She mounted the three steps of the catafalque, and stood for some minutes before the coffin, repeating the words, 'thirty-five years ... thirty-five years'.

On the day of the funeral, 5th June, we had a choir practice at 9am, and then I changed into my morning suit, and made my way up Denton's Commons through a maze of opulent cars, BBC vans, uniformed and morning-suited officials. The vestry bell rang, and we filed into Chapel, and up into the organ loft. Whereas at one time we had a full view of the proceedings, we had now to be content to take a discreet peep through the curtains. The scene down below was one of solemnity and splendour. King Olaf of Norway walked with the Duke of Edinburgh, followed by the Prince of Wales. The Duchess of Windsor sat with the Queen, and I thought how frail and slight she looked. Many celebrities sat in our lay clerks' stalls, including Harold Wilson, Alec Douglas-Home, and Jeremy Thorpe. The Prime Minister, Edward Heath, sat near the Sanctuary, and of his interest in the music there could have been no doubt. He was, of course an Organ Scholar in his Oxford days.

The service, which was quite simple and was broadcast, included Croft's *Burial Sentences*, Wesley's *Thou wilt keep him in perfect peace*, and two hymns: *The King of Love* and *Lead us, Heavenly Father*. Psalm 90 was sung as meticulously as I have ever heard it. Dr Sidney Campell was at the organ, and conducted the unaccompanied singing. The Last Post and Reveille were played from the bottom of the nave by the State Trumpeters of the Household Cavalry.

The *Guardian* observed: 'The silver thunder of the trumpets sounding "Last Post" and "Reveille" drowned the aircraft rumbles that even the St George's Chapel organ had been unable to conquer'. The service was conducted by the Dean of Windsor, and the Blessing was given by the Archbishop of Canterbury, Dr Ramsey. The dead Duke's Styles and Titles were proclaimed by the Garter Principal King of Arms, Sir Anthony Wagner.

At the end of the service, members of the Royal Family curtsied or bowed before the coffin as they filed out. The Interment was private and took place at Frogmore, and as I went up the Long Walk later, I caught the flash of limousines through the trees. After Evensong that day the Dean told the choir that the singing at the funeral had been greatly appreciated, particularly by the Queen, who sent us a personal message of thanks, and also lovely roses to all who had taken part. We all thought the singing had gone well, and it would appear that the organ loft has its advantages acoustically. The acoustics in the nave of St George's are superb, but the choir is not so resonant, owing to the many banners and heavy woodwork.

IV *The Garter Service*

There is one annual event at Windsor which has its own unique place in the national calendar. This is the 'Garter Service', held in June, when new Knights of the Most Noble Order of the Garter are installed. This ceremony is only exceeded in pomp and pageantry by a Coronation, and thousands of visitors flock to the Castle to watch the procession of Knights in their magnificent robes.

The Order of the Garter was founded in 1348 by Edward III – who also greatly improved the amenities of the Castle. 'No Order in Europe', it has been said, 'is so ancient, none so illustrious, for it exceeds in majesty, honour and fame, all Chivalrous Fraternities in the World'.[1] Although that may sound strange to modern ears, one may, perhaps, still preserve the general concept of 'chivalry'.

I took part in many Garter Services, and witnessed the installation of many famous men as Knights of the Garter. Among them was Sir Winston Churchill in 1954, when he was still Prime Minister. I described the occasion in my diary:

> Before the service commenced, the choir processed to the west end of the nave to await the arrival of the Knights. These waits are always long and tedious, but any discomfort is trivial when compared with the length of time the guards lining the Chapel steps outside have to endure. Several of them just collapsed from the heat, and as each one keeled over there was a gasp from the crowds, and murmurs of sympathy as they were carried away. At last the procession headed by the Military Knights reached the Chapel steps, at which point the choir turned and moved eastward through the choir screen into their stalls. One by one the Garter Knights moved into the stalls, and behind them came Queen Elizabeth the Queen Mother and the Duke of Gloucester, followed by the Officers of the Order. Finally came the Queen with her pages holding her splendid robes, and the Duke of Edinburgh. The new Knight to be installed was Sir Winston Churchill. I was quite near to him as he leaned against the choirboys' stalls, and it was a touching moment when the young Queen said: 'It is our pleasure that the Knight Companion be installed'. The Garter King of Arms, Sir George Bellew, then conducted Sir Winston to his stall. It was moving to see the old man, now in his eightieth year – pull himself slowly and heavily up the stall. The glorious colours, pageantry and fanfares made it a truly memorable occasion.

At another Garter Service a year or two later, I turned to watch the Knights processing into the stalls, and as Sir Winston took up his

---

[1] See H W Blackburne and M F Bond, *The Romance of St George's*, revised edition 1962; foreword by E K C Hamilton, Dean of Windsor, London, 1962.

place behind me, he caught my eye. He leaned forward, and I found myself looking rather embarrassingly into his great round pink face. 'It's hot in here', he said, 'can you do anything about it?' I muttered something like: 'I wish I could, Sir.' Turning to Clement Attlee, he said quite loudly: 'Can *you* do anything about it?' He replied with an inaudible grunt! As the Service was drawing to a close, I heard behind me: 'Phew, I say, how much longer is this going on?'

My wife always put on a lavish buffet for our many guests. These feasts became legendary, and regarded by all as a special feature to round off Garter days as viewed from the Hodgson household. On one occasion, Sir Edwin Leather, MP (later Governor of Burmuda), was a guest, and shortly after I went with a quartet to sing at a dinner in London. As I entered the room, I heard a voice said: 'Ah – Freddy Hodgson, his wife makes wonderful sandwiches.' It was Sir Ted Leather!

Apart from the great occasions, a lay clerk at Windsor is called on from time to time to take part in more intimate, family ceremonies. There is a small private chapel in the Royal Apartments which nowadays is used mainly for services on Good Fridays, and for christenings, etc. Services are attended by the Royal Family and their staff, and the choir consists of a few boys and three lay clerks from St George's Chapel, who sing from a cream and gold balcony, which formerly was a royal pew. At one time lay clerks used the additional title of 'Gentlemen of HM Private Chapel in Windsor Castle'. (The Private Chapel, including the organ, was completely destroyed in the great fire at Windsor Castle in November, 1992. The organ, built by Henry Willis in 1889, had two four-manual consoles, one in St George's Hall, and the other in the Private Chapel.)

One service at which I sang was the Confirmation of Prince Charles in April 1965. The Archbishop of Canterbury, Dr Ramsey, officiated, and it was a solemn moment when he placed his hands on the young Prince's head. In his sermon, the Primate asked the Prince to remember these words: 'O God, my heart is ready', and he requested the congregation to repeat these words, which were so significant for a future monarch. A practical musician himself, he has always shown an interest in the music at St George's, and once when the Queen sent a brace of pheasants to each lay clerk in appreciation of their work over Christmas, the birds were specially selected by the Prince, and they were superb. Cloisters residents have also been the recipients of beautiful roses from the Queen.

CHAPTER NINE
Officers of the Chapel

The Dean of Windsor, Bishop Eric Hamilton, died in 1962, and was succeeded by the Ven Robin Woods, Archdeacon of Sheffield, whom I had known since he was a young man. He was the son of the Rt Rev E S Woods, Bishop of Lichfield. He proved to be an excellent dean, and soon made his presence felt, and was on Christian-name terms with us all. St George's House, now known nationally for its conferences involving people from all walks of life, came to fruition through his initiative and drive. The venture had the enthusiastic support of Prince Philip, and the House was dedicated by the Queen in 1966. At the Dedication Service, Robin Woods was described in a sermon by the Precentor as 'a turbulent priest who has driven everyone to bring this thing to pass'. He had a voice strikingly similar to that of his father, of a particularly powerful and resonant timbre characteristic of the Woods family. One day as I sat in my house, I distinctly heard every word he said as he talked to a group outside on the Chapel steps! On another occasion I was driving through Newport in Pembrokeshire, where the dean had a cottage, when I stopped the car and put my head out of the window. My wife Bethy looked puzzled. 'What's the matter, why have you stopped?' she asked. 'It's OK, don't worry,' I replied, 'the dean's here on holiday, and I am wondering if I would hear him.' It was a matter of great regret when he left us in 1971 to become Bishop of Worcester. He certainly left his mark on St George's, and injected some life into the place, and was generally considered to be pretty dynamic. As a Bishop he did not hesitate to express his convictions, irrespective of whether they were popular or not. The three canons now were G B Bentley, J A Fisher and R H Hawkins. Canon Bentley had succeeded Canon Venables as Precentor, and his expertise on ritual and ceremonial was soon in evidence. Canon Fisher was an eloquent preacher, and Canon Hawkins came with a wealth of experience as a parish priest, and was a former Vicar of Nottingham. I got to know him well, and we often walked up the 'Hundred Steps' together, which lead from the bottom of Thames Street to the Canons' Cloisters. One day, as we started ascending these steps, I told him I practised rhythmic breathing when climbing steps. He said he would try it, and we both completed the ascent by breathing in for three steps, holding the breath for the next three, and exhaling for the next three, regularly in that order until we reached the top, with neither of us the least bit out of breath. The Canon was still going up those steps rhythmically and effortlessly years later, when he was in his eighties.

There was a succession of excellent minor canons in Revs Gordon Dunstan (afterwards Canon Dunstan, Professor of Moral and Social Theology at King's College, London, with whom I later became associated at the Chapel Royal, St James's Palace, where he was Priest-in-Ordinary, and is now a Chaplain to the Queen), David Galliford (afterwards Bishop of Bolton), Douglas Bean, John Nourse, Timothy Hine, Donald Fehrenbach, and latterly Ian Collins (now Canon of Southwell), and John Crane. In 1960, a new and dedicated verger appeared in Roy Read, who maintained a particularly high standard in that office.

The end of an era occurred in 1961 with the retirement of Sir William Harris, at the age of 78. He had been organist since 1933, and had achieved a monumental position in English church music. He was an organist and a prolific composer of church music. His anthem *Faire is the Heaven* is an established classic. He brought to his work a dignity and refinement not always met with nowadays. His choir training was austere, rigid, and free of gimmicks. He could be extremely difficult, and he had a positive obsession about intonation. He would not hesitate to give a corrective 'peep' on the organ if he thought someone had strayed off the note, and this was not always accepted without strong protests from minor canons and lay clerks. (Russell Thorndike, who was chorister at St George's in the latter years of Queen Victoria, recalls in his memoirs, *Children of the Garter*, how Sir Walter Parratt would correct any drop in pitch by a blast 'upon the tuba stop on the great organ. He would stump about the organ loft, tearing his hair, and shaking his fists in full view of the congregation'). But he could also be very kindly, and I had many friendly chats with him, often late in the evening; on occasion he would ask me to sing songs, and his piano accompaniments were delightful. He did not approve of anything which might be detrimental to my voice. 'Don't use your voice too much in schools', he would say, and once he came hurrying out of his house to ask me why I was cleaning my car on such a bitterly cold day.

Not long before he retired, he told me that Prince Philip and Benjamin Britten had been in the organ loft with him at morning service. 'The Duke has asked Benjamin Britten to write something for St George's choir', he said. 'I wonder what it will be like? I hope it will be alright'. The result was a striking *Jubilate* in C major, which is now so well known. Its first performance was given at St George's in July, 1961, and Sir William was so enthusiastic about it that he wrote to the *Musical Times* to say that we had been honoured by giving it its first performance; so it must have been 'alright!' In one of my last conversations with him he said: 'I am taking away with me a great collection of records. I keep them all in here', he added, as he tapped his head. He and Lady Harris retired to Petersfield, where he died in 1973, at the age of 90.

The organistship of St George's is, of course, one that carries particular prestige, and there was much speculation as to a successor to Sir William Harris. The appointment went eventually to Dr Sidney Campbell, organist of Canterbury Cathedral. His career had been meteoric, coming up to St George's via West Ham Parish Church, St Peter's, Croydon, St Peter's Collegiate Church, Wolverhampton, and Ely, Southwark and Canterbury Cathedrals. He was also Sub Warden and Director of Studies at the Royal School of Church Music. I first met him in 1946 at Lichfield, when he came to the Cathedral to conduct at a Diocesan Festival. He told me he was wearing his Doctor's robes for the first time on that occasion.

His methods of choir training were highly individual, and in complete contrast to those of his predecessor. He was something of an actor, and he had his own inimitable way of illustrating a point, for example in music with a martial rhythm, or which had a succession of staccato chords, which would always get special treatment. 'Imagine you are a little French Bandmaster', he would say, drawing himself up with a feigned pomposity ... 'waxed moustache, baton, brass buttons, and all'. He would then walk stiffly and mechanically across the Song School Floor, wielding an imaginary baton. Like this ... 'O – praise – the – Lord – laud – ye – the – name – of – the – Lord!' He would then look round quizzically, and say: 'I am quite unpredictable, so don't be surprised at anything I do or say.'

Sidney Campbell had a real sense of humour, but his practices could, according to mood, range from the hilarious to the tensely edgy and uncomfortable, and an abrupt and premature termination of a practice was not unknown. He came into the Song School one morning and told the choir he had not slept well. 'I have a geyser upstairs', he said, implying that it made a noise. 'An old 'un or a young 'un?' someone murmured. He was quick to appreciate any joke.

Once we were singing the word 'Hallelujah', when he said he would like the third syllable to be accented. 'Come down heavily on the "lu",' he said, and then joined in the uproar. I once told him the story related to me by my old Lichfield colleague, William Wood, of how when he was at Christ Church, Oxford, the genial C H Lloyd would come into the vestry, and say jocularly: 'Good morning, gentlemen and altos'. He was vastly amused, and he said: 'In future I shall call you gentlemen altos', and that is how he always addressed us.

He was something of a 'loner', highly strung and very nervous, and he once said to me: 'I don't know how I got through practice this morning, I had what Gordon Reynolds described as that organist's feeling of impending doom.' He was a flamboyant character, tall and thin, with a whimsical, puckish face. The way in which he dressed gave further insight into his personality. I shall always picture him wearing a beret, bow-tie and long 'camel' coat. He was a virtuoso recitalist, and an authoritative exponent of French organ music. He had a predilection for baroque organs (definitely not shared by his predecessor, Sir William Harris) which no doubt influenced his somewhat controversial views on vocal tone, which he equated with instrumental sounds. There is nothing new in that, but when it is over-emphasised it does raise the question as to which came first, instruments or voices? He would describe a voice as an 'oboe' voice, or a French horn voice, etc. He supervised the rebuilding of the organ by Harrison, of Durham, which was opened in June 1965, in the presence of the Queen Mother at the Festival Evensong of the Friends of St George's, at the end of which service he gave a demonstration of the new instrument in Bach's *Toccata and Fugue in D minor*.

When relaxed, Campbell was loquacious and – having a phenomenal memory – would recall personalities and repeat conversations of many years ago verbatim. A bachelor, he lived alone in Dr Fellowes's old house. One night, as he was in his kitchen washing up, some lay clerks in high spirits were passing his house, when suddenly one of them let forth a terrific sustained top A. Immediately there was a crashing sound of broken crockery, and Sidney Campbell, looking startled, appeared at the door on his shirt sleeves. 'Whoever that was made me drop a plate', he said. He was never very robust and in latter years his health began to fail. He died suddenly in 1974 at the age of 65 after being organist for 13 years. He was succeeded by Christopher Robinson, Organist of Worcester Cathedral, who raised the music to a superlatively high standard.[1]

At one time lay clerks never left St George's; they were there for life. From 1895 to 1956 only six alto appointments were made, and very few tenors and basses. As a widely sought-after layclerkship there has been no lack of candidates, and in my time some notable appointments were made. Albert Key and Archie Cooper were succeeded by two excellent tenors, Philip Howell and Gordon Fowler, and in 1956 an alto from Exeter Cathedral, Perceval Bridger, succeeded Wallis Searle. He had a voice with a remarkable upper reigster. He was a fine portrait painter too, and altogether a personality. He died very suddenly in 1970. Latterly I had excellent new alto colleagues in Brian Northcott (formerly at Tenbury) and two from King's College, Cambridge, in Nigel Perrin, who became one of The King's Singers, and Alan Kendall, author of notable biographies on Vivaldi, Beethoven, Rossini, Tchaikovsky, Boulanger, Gershwin and Britten. There were also Derek McCulloch, lecturer at the University of Surrey, and Nigel Dixon, of The Scholars. Three fine young bass colleagues in recent years were Graham Sorrell — later of St Paul's — Timothy Rowe and Mervyn Bryn Jones.

In a long list of musicians who have served St George's well, not least in importance were some of the assistant organists. Without a cooperative, efficient and reliable assistant, the work of a cathedral organist would be well nigh impossible. Assistants usually have the full support of their organists, who delegate authority. Very seldom is this abused, though I have known instances of abuse of delegated authority. The assistant acts as a liaison with the choir, with which there is usually a good relationship. When I arrived in 1951 Lionel Dakers was the assistant. He became successively organist of Ripon

---

[1] Christopher Robinson was appointed Organist of St John's College, Cambridge, in 1991. He was succeeded at St George's by Jonathan Rees-Williams, Organist of Lichfield Cathedral.

and Exeter Cathedrals, and was Director of the Royal School of Church Music from 1972 to 1989, in which office he exerted a powerful influence over church music throughout the English-speaking world.

Among earlier assistants of outstanding merit was Malcolm Boyle, later organist of Chester Cathedral. The son of a renowned lay clerk of St George's, he was himself a chorister at Eton College. After a brilliant career as a student at the Royal Academy of Music, he distinguished himself greatly as assistant at St George's in the interregnum between Parratt's death in 1924 and Walford Davies's arrival in 1927. During this period Dr Fellowes acted as choirmaster. H C Colles in his book *Walford Davies* (OUP, 1942) says:

> Walford's engagement books of the first years at Windsor seem to be quite as full of distant engagements as were those before he got there. Mr. Malcolm Boyle must have had almost as much playing of daily services to do after Walford's arrival as before, and the maintenance of daily choral services is the first purpose for which the musical establishment of the Chapel is provided.

Malcolm Boyle was an organist of outstanding ability, and I spent many an Evensong with him in the organ loft at Chester. He was genial and humorous, and he would chat away to me of his days at Windsor as he went on accompanying most of the service from memory. (Another friend who could perform this feat with equal aplomb was Dr Osborne Peasgood, sub-organist of Westminster Abbey for many years. 'Ossy' would play through a service perfectly, and at the same time be reading a motoring magazine propped up in front of him). The anthem at Chester one day was Brahms's *How lovely is Thy dwelling place* from the *German Requiem*. With no copy in sight, Malcolm turned to me saying: 'I think I'll play it in E major − it sounds better'. In its original E flat this movement makes demands on the upper alto register, and I pointed out that by transposing it up the altos would have to have to go up to top E. 'That's no problem here', he replied. 'You know that Jack Hawkins will really enjoy it.' Jack, a former pupil of mine and a life-long friend, was a noted Chester alto. After Malcolm's death in 1976 at the age of 74, his former chorister at Chester Cathedral, Dr George Guest, organist of St John's College, Cambridge, wrote an obituary notice, which is reprinted here by kind permission of Dr Guest. It is, perhaps, symbolic of the affection which Malcolm inspired that

Dr Guest travelled north specially to play the organ at the village church at Sandiway in Cheshire where the funeral service took place:

It is not easy to write briefly about one so universally loved and admired as Malcolm Boyle, even for those of us fortunate enough to come under his influence as cathedral choristers.

It has been said that the essence of a conductor's personality and perhaps his character can be seen in his rehearsals. MCB's way at rehearsals was the way of reason and this, coupled with an approach as compassionate as it was courteous, enabled him to achieve results which were often the envy of his colleagues. His extraordinary talent, his sunny personality and his supreme optimism (even in the face of dire personal anxiety) were magnets which drew young and old alike.

As an organist (he was a former pupil of Sir Walter Parratt) he was quite superb in his interpretation of the great works of the Romantic era. Composers like Liszt, Rheinberger, Reubke and others took their turn with J S Bach to be represented at the end of the Sunday 3.30 pm Evensong. And the South Transept was usually full of people who knew they were listening to music that came as much from the heart as from the fingers and feet. His improvisations were products of genius, models of such construction, and many a time did a visitor wait at the bottom of the organ-loft steps to ask the name of the piece. At the end of his last service as cathedral organist he improvised a masterly voluntary of heart-rending poignancy, based, characteristically, on the intonation to the creed.

Malcolm Boyle won friends in all walks of life. He had a never-ending fund of anecdotes which brought to life his days as a chorister at Eton College, his association with Parratt, E H Fellowes, and Sir Walford Davies, and his early days at Chester Cathedral. This great gift of being able to communicate easily with people made him an ideal examiner for the Associated Board of the Royal Schools of Music, and the popular adjudicator at music festivals in many parts of the world.

The passing of MCB leaves a gap in the ranks of cathedral musicians, but his name will live on in the hearts of his pupils and friends and his compositions, which are small in number but of characteristic beauty.

Two other distinguished cathedral organists who were former assistants at St George's were Alwyn Surplice, organist of Bristol and Winchester cathedrals, and Richard Greening, of Lichfield. Others in the list include John Forster, Philip Moore (Head of Music, BBC Bristol), Clement MacWilliam, John Morehen, Professor of Music at Nottingham University and editor of church music, and John Porter, who first came to Windsor as an organ scholar, and then became assistant Roger Judd became assistant organist of St George's in 1986, having previously been organist of St Michael's College, Tenbury for twelve years up to the time of its closure in 1985, which saw the disbandment of a choir of outstanding excellence.

CHAPTER TEN
Variety of life in a castle setting

'Are there any ghosts in Windsor Castle?' That is one question which crops up with almost monotonous regularity! There are, of course, many stories of apparitions and strange happenings, as there are in respect of any ancient building around which legends have accumulated. Speaking personally I must say (confessing at the same time that I am no more immune from the influence of legends – especially the sort that get televised) that from time to time I have been uneasy, particularly late at night when looking for the cat. It may very well have been imagination at work, but I once at least felt positive that it was not the wind in the Castle walls, but groans that I heard, from the direction of the Curfew Tower dungeons, where prisoners were once held – some until the time of their execution. It is said that Anne Boleyn spent some time there.

Quite late one night my son John came in and said excitedly, 'Dad, there are voices coming from the Curfew Tower.' I went outside with him, and we stood by the Tower railings, and sure enough, there were voices! After a moment's breathless listening we both grinned, with relief perhaps, as we realised that the voices were coming from the Tower-keeper's radio! I wondered afterwards if John had been pulling my leg ...

Other experiences were not so easily explained, such as the one when I was in the Long Walk at dusk, when I noticed a woman walking towards me dressed all in white, with a close-fitting hat reminiscent of the 1920s, and she was swinging a large white handbag. I felt my hair tingle as there was no sound of footsteps, and she passed by in complete silence. When I could summon up enough courage, I turned and looked backward and scanned the wide open grass spaces, and she was nowhere to be seen. When I retraced my steps and hurried down the Walk, it was completely deserted.

The Long Walk is often enveloped in mists, which can develop very quickly, and one night, as I found myself groping through one of these, I heard the approach of horse hooves which alarmed me as they seemed to be coming straight at me. I then caught sight dimly of a figure on a horse galloping past me with what appeared to be hair streaming. My first impression was that the rider was a woman, but afterwards I wondered. My perhaps too vivid imagination ran riot, and I had visions of the centuries-old legend of Herne the Hunter, who was said to be a horned demon which haunted Windsor Forest, and described by Shakespeare in *The Merry Wives of Windsor*:

> There is an old tale goes that Herne the Hunter,
> Sometime a keeper here in Windsor Forest,
> Doth all the winter time, at still midnight,
> Walk round about an oak, with grear ragg'd horns,
> And there he blasts the tree ...

There have been many sightings of the demon hunter riding in the forest, and a strange incident which occurred on the East Terrace of Windsor Castle in October, 1976, brings him to mind. A young Coldstream Guardsman on duty in the middle of the night was found unconscious by his relief, and had to be taken to hospital. He explained to his officer that he was looking at a statue when horns appeared on it and it came to life. There are other stories of sentries on Castle duty who have had ghostly experiences, and it is said that many years ago a guard on duty on a bitter winter's night saw a cloaked figure approaching him. He was so terrified that he fired at the figure, narrowly missing it. But it turned out to be the Dean, who in his kindness had taken the soldier a bowl of hot gruel. He got 20 lashes!

Extraneous noises during services at St George's are commonplace. The stentorian bellowings of Guardsmen on the parade ground often vie discordantly with the music, and the roar of jets overhead has destroyed many a *pianissimo* and caused lessons being read to cease suddenly until the 'tyranny be overpast'.

During the building of the King George the Sixth Memorial Chapel in 1969, the first architectural enlargement to St George's since 1504, designed by George Pace, and completed in nine months, a large number of workmen were employed, and their bangings and hammerings were often to be heard during services. When the choir is lined up in the North choir aisle ready for service, it is an ancient custom for the verger to call out in a loud voice the words 'Toll's down', signifying that the bells in the Curfew Tower have ceased to ring.

One morning during the building of the Memorial Chapel, 'Toll's down' was immediately answered by a tremendous shout from a workman outside – 'Tea's up'. Canon Hawkins, who was about to say a prayer, joined in the laughter!

Residents of Windsor Castle see members of the Royal Family frequently in the precincts, and they are also to be seen driving up the Long Walk on their way to Ascot, Royal Lodge, or Smith's Lawn. Royal cars are eagerly awaited by tourists, who stand by the Castle gates, particularly in Ascot Week. A delightful story is told of two small children who were out walking with their parents in the Long Walk. The children ran on far head up the Walk, while their parents strolled leisurely behind. When the little ones were almost out of sight, a storm suddenly sprang up, and it started to rain torrentially. There is a long avenue of trees, but they offer only slight protection, and the children were beyond these, out in the open, and but two tiny dots in the distance. The Walk was deserted, except for a car driven by Prince Philip, which sped by towards the castle. The only thing the parents could do was to shelter under a tree, and wait anxiously until the soaked and bedraggled children came running up to t iem. 'A man pulled up in a car', they said, 'and asked where we wer ? going, and would we like a lift down the Walk. But we said no, thank you, we are not allowed to accept lifts from strangers!'

Another story of Prince Philip was told to me some years ago by a Windsor barber, who was a Yorkshireman with the broadest of accents. He was a first-class barber, patronised by many castle residents. As he started to snip away at my hair, he said confidentially: 'I cut t'Dook's hair last night. His barber was ill, and they sent for me, and by goom I was scared to death. I was shown into a grand room, and in comes t'Dook. He must have seen I was a bit nervous like, and he started to chat right friendly, and by t'time I had t'sheet round his neck, I felt fine. He was such a gentleman, and he only wanted a trim. But what amazed me was when he said: "You come from Yorkshire" ... 'ow the 'ell did he know?'

During the restoration of the Cloisters in 1963, it became necessary for us to vacate our house, No 12A, while the work went on. We moved temporarily to No 25, a large rambling house of great character, commanding superb views over the Thames. It was formerly the home of Canon Dalton, father of Hugh Dalton, a former Chancellor of the Exchequer, who was brought up in the house. When Sir Walford

Davies was organist, he and Lady Davies occupied the house. It is in that part of the Cloisters known as Denton's Commons, after a former Canon, and contains fragments of the Great Hall of King Henry the Third's Palace. Major restoration of the house in 1965 uncovered superb scissor-beam roof trusses of the 13th century, and a cylindrical chimney (c 1170). The first-floor bedroom, when stripped of plaster, revealed a 14/15th-century fireplace, over which there were remains of plainsong notation. A 13th-century doorway was also uncovered. It is thought that these may have been the royal chambers used by Henry the Third, and in the 14th century it is very likely they were lodgings for priests and clerks of St George's. During our six months' residence there my colleagues would greet me with a mock bow, and a 'good morning, "Canon" Hodgson', which could be interpreted either as a promotion or a doubtful compliment! Although we enjoyed the space and grace of living there, it was a cold house, and very expensive to run; we were glad to return to our old house in the Horseshoe Cloisters, which now looked magnificent after its restoration, and my wife's tasteful refurnishing.

Although my family and I remained on excellent terms with all Cloisters residents for so many years, and despite the glamour of such an environment, we found living in Windsor Castle was like living in a goldfish bowl. The never-ending multitudes of tourists created an absolute lack of privacy, and we often had to push our way through crowds to enter our house. In spite of notices saying that the grass was for residents only, deckchairs belonging to residents, if left unoccupied for a moment on the cloister lawn, were likely to be commandeered by strangers. Our house was on the route to the Curfew Tower, and to leave a window or door open was to invite many a head to come peering in, and on numerous occasions strangers have even walked into the house. One day, my wife Bethy had been conducting a party of women friends round the castle, and as they all trooped back into the house for tea, another party of strangers tagged on and entered the house. Bethy gently and discreetly asked who they were, and what could she do for them. They then realised that they were trespassing, but explained that they thought it was part of an officially conducted tour. Their embarrassment was relieved when Bethy treated it as a huge joke, and in due course the intruders departed in good humour.

Children of the Cloisters now enjoy a greater freedom than did their more immediate predecessors. Ball-games take place on the lawn, and cycles flash along the walks, and there is a cheerful chatter of children's voices. One can imagine the repressions of a century ago in the words of Dean Wellesley:[1]

> To your own promise be true,
> No damage to turf, or noise undue.

The notion that a cat may look at a queen was, maybe, first developed in the precincts of Windsor Castle, where there has never been a dearth of cats. Among them I recall an outstanding character belonging to us who spent the whole of his 15 years within the grey walls of the castle.

'Chuck' was a magnificent animal, with a marmalade-coloured coat, and he had a characteristic 'M' mark between an incredibly large pair of golden eyes. He retained this pretty kitten face throughout his life. As will appear, we thought he was musical.

He was the most docile of animals, though in his youth he was something of a hunter, and he was soon attracted to the birds and small animals in the Home Park, and on the slopes of the Round Tower. My younger son, Chris, and I used to go in search of him nearly every night, and he would appear out of the darkness at the sound of our familiar 'phut-phut' calls. But if he was in one of his fey moods he would come almost within our grasp, and then suddenly dart away through the locked gates of the North Terrace; on occasion an amused policeman would come to our aid with a key. He kept up this exasperating practise for years. When finally rounded up, Chris would drape him round his shoulders and carry him home.

One evening a Military Knight, looking through his window in the Lower Ward, saw what he thought was a 'suspicious character' carrying a sack over his shoulder. He at once telephoned the Castle police, who soon reassured him that it was only young Chris carrying home his cat.

I was looking for him one summer evening when Lord Freyburg, VC, came up to me enquiringly, and I explained I was looking for 'Chuck'. The famous soldier pointed to the Round Tower slopes and said: 'He's up there stalking mice. He's a great campaigner, and I often watch him'. On another occasion, a guard standing at attention saw me looking around and, to avoid speaking to me directly while on duty, he hissed out of the side of his mouth: 'He's in that bush; he's been rubbing round my _____ legs!'

[1] Gerald Wellesley, a nephew of the Duke of Wellington, was Dean of Windsor from 1854–82.

In support of the looking-at-the-queen theory, 'Chuck' was reported on one occasion at least to have made his way into the Royal Apartments – if not into the innermost sanctum, at least into the kitchens. Quite shameless, he would frequently perform noctural serenades on the East Terrace together with one of his intimate friends. He was particularly attracted to St George's Chapel, where he would slink in unnoticed, and he would often follow choir processions through the Cloisters. Before any ceremonial occasion he had to be rounded up and shut away safely in the house, for he had inevitably – it seemed – previous warning of anything ceremonial out-of doors. No cat could have claimed to have weaved in and out of so many famous legs: After one state funeral, mourners were walking along the outside path of the Chapel viewing the long line of wreaths when there to ad l a touch of comedy to a sad occasion was 'Chuck', heading the procession and paying his last respects by sniffing each wreath in turn. One Good Friday morning I was on Private Chapel duty, and as I was walking through St George's Hall on my way to the Chapel, a Castle policeman came hurrying after me. Pointing behind me, he said: 'Here, is *he* going to sing too?' I turned, and there was 'Chuck', who had followed me, and I was unaware of it. As it was almost time for rehearsal, I had to grab him, and dash back home with him!

Chuck could claim to be one of the most photographed of cats, and his picture must grace many a collection; he was fondled and admired by countless tourists. An abiding memory was to see him sitting in the Cloisters waiting for members of the family to come home. We considered him to have a particularly good ear, for in spite of the constant stream of cars coming and going, it was uncanny how he would recognise the different engine sounds of our family cars, often in the dark, and he would run towards them with howls of joy. Often when I met him, it was a ritual for him to slide his wet nose up my face as I bent towards him, and he would push off my hat or cap, to the vast amusement of tourists.

Living within the sound of choral and organ music, as well as ceremonial fanfares, military bands and the chimes and peals of the Curfew Tower, and educated (so to speak) in domestic music-making, 'Chuck' could claim among cats to be distinguished as a musical authority. During choir practices he would sit outside the Song School. One morning Sidney Campbell noticed that the boys were distracted by something that was capturing their attention outside the window. 'Boys', he said sharply, 'what's going on out there? Pay attention.' 'Mr Hodgson's cat wants him', one boy − rather bolder than the rest − said.

When Chris played the piano the cat would jump on his knee to provide an independent motif, by pawing individual notes, from which he would develop virtuoso passages by discovering that the instrument for him was available for both manual and pedal techniques. He has been known to give solo performances in the middle of the night. It will be remembered that Scarlatti's *Katzenfugue* was inspired by his cat walking across the keyboard of his harpsichord, as was Chopin's *Cat Valse*. But 'Chuck' hated noise, and would cringe and cry if anyone whistled shrilly, and the roar of a jet plane would send him indoors crawling on his belly, with his ears flattened. John would subject him to what he called a *Trumpet* or *Trombone Treadle*, in which he held him in one hand while he worked a hind leg backwards and forwards with the other as he strode up and down the room humming Purcell's *Trumpet Tune*. 'Chuck' never once objected to this. But his party piece, much appreciated by visitors to the house, was to see him on a cold day walk to an electric fire and warm his face with a rotating motion, and then turn round and elevate his rump and do likewise!

The day came when the vet sadly pronounced the death sentence, and 'Chuck' made a both dignified and pathetic figure when, for the last time, he staggered into the Cloisters. The last sounds he heard were the Curfew Tower bells. Sentimentality over a mere cat, or just another pampered animal, it may be thought. But 'Chuck' was no ordinary cat. He was an aristocrat among cats, and lived like a king. He walked in the path of kings, and certainly graced his royal environment. He was generally acknowledged to be a lovable and unusual character, and we are grateful for the pleasure he gave to us and others for so many years.

'Are there', ask the tourists, 'any ghosts in Windsor Castle?'

But 'Chuck' lives on in the painting of the Garter Procession by Sir Terence Cuneo, which was commissioned by the Queen in 1964, and now hangs in the Chapter Library of Windsor Castle. The famous artist worked from a position on the Cloisters lawn, facing the West Front of St George's Chapel. This was 'Chuck's' territory, and he attracted the attention of the artist, who included him in the picture. He can be seen behind the figure of a Military Knight. A cat in the picture complements the artist's famous logo − a mouse!

CHAPTER ELEVEN
Male-voice singing

Singing by men's voices has always been one of my greatest pleasures. To quote William Byrd again: 'There is not any musicke of instruments comparable to that which is made of the voyces of men, when the voices are good, and the same well-sorted and ordered.' As well as singing the regular repertoire of services and anthems for men's voices in cathedrals and chapels. I have always had a complementary vocation as a member of a male-voice ensemble. I began to practise this social art in Sheffield, and am still committed to it.

My long and memorable association with the Lichfield Cathedral Quartet provided some amusing and anxious moments. Our activities were varied, and we travelled extensively. We had a large repertoire, all of which we had committed to memory. Our journeys were usually made in Albert Hodkinson's car, and one day during a thunderstorm we suffered a punctured tyre. It was summertime and we had set out in sunshine and a clear sky, and we had no raincoats. We couldn't very well leave Albert to change the tyre unaided, so we got out into the deluge to give a hand. The effect on our dinner dress was devastating. We were quickly soaked through, we got grease on our shirt fronts and cuffs from handling the spare wheel and the jack, and must have looked a dejected and bedraggled lot when we arrived at our destination in Birmingham just in time to perform. But after explaining to the audience we were given a sympathetic and appreciative reception. One item in the programme was Elgar's *As torrents in summer* which we sang with appropriate gestures, thereby causing much merriment.

On another occasion in Albert's car we were accompanied by his wife and two large dogs, who were shedding their coats. We all sat crammed and uncomfortable with the boisterous animals pawing and scrambling all over us, and the fur really began to fly. When we got out of the car we were horrified to see our suits thickly covered in white and brown dog-hairs. We had been engaged to sing at a civic dinner in the Potteries, and we arrived with only a few minutes to spare before we were due to sing the Grace. After some frantic and futile hair-picking (there is nothing more tenacious than dog hairs on a dinner jacket), we faced a distinguished audience with some embarrassment, feeling like four shaggy dogs!

Herbert Parker objected to any form of conducting when we sang, but occasionally Albert felt that a beat was necessary, and once during a broadcast he began to conduct. This was too much for Herbert, who gesticulated for him to stop with downward movements of his hand. But Albert continued to the bitter end, and so did Herbert, which merely produced two conflicting beats. As we were on the air, the situation was hazardous, but mercifully the tempo was not affected unduly.

Shortly after going to Windsor, I began to sing with a number of male-voice groups in London, and for many years it has been my pleasure to sing as a member of a quartet with such renowned singers as Alfred Hepworth and Kenneth Tudor, both of Westminster Abbey, and Stanley Riley, formerly of St Paul's Cathedral, the Chapel Royal and the BBC Singers. (The late lamented Kenneth Tudor has not only left abiding memories of his magnificent bass voice and much admired personality, but also as the humorist of the Abbey choir. Anecdotes of his antics in and out of the choir stalls are legendary). The venue of our rehearsals has varied from song-schools to trains, cars, buses, corridors, or wherever convenient. But talking of convenience reminds me of occasions when we had nowhere to rehearse before a performance at the Connaught Rooms, except down in the palatial toilets, where the tiled walls give an added resonance, and the plumbing tends to provide its own mellifluous accompaniment. Audiences of elegant gentlemen have gathered and thanked us warmly for an unexpected post-ablutionary concert!

At a dinner in Westminster School, held in the superb 12th-century candle-lit dining room, a rather alarming incident occurred as Stanley Riley was singing *Here's to the maiden*, a song for which he is famous. When he arrived at the chorus − 'Let the toast pass, drink to the lass' − a school servant, stealthily carrying a huge tray packed with bottles and glasses, tripped and down came the tray with a tremendous crash, leaving Stanley in the middle of the debris. But with glass in hand, and with his usual *sang froid*, he continued his fine singing, and soon had the shocked audience laughing, cheering and joining in the chorus.

At one time every cathedral had its quartet, and most towns could muster a male-voice choir. But nowadays it seems that, apart from the established choirs in Wales and a few others mostly in the north and Cornwall, male-voice singing is on the decline. It is true that there are several sophisticated and highly professional groups such as The King's Singers, and there have also been some desultory attempts to reproduce the 'barber shop' style of singing since its fashionable revival in the United States, where it is now recognised as an authentic form of folk music.

One of the remaining bastions of male-voice singing in this country is the City Glee Club, London. This exclusive club has behind it a tradition of 300 years, as when it was re-established in 1853 it was a reconstruction of the so-called Civil Club founded in 1669 in the reign of Charles II. Many distinguished members of parliament, Baronets and Aldermen of the City of London have been among its members. The Lord Mayor of London is the Honorary President, and the Dean of Westminster is Honorary Chaplain. The performances are entrusted to professional singers, drawn mainly from the choirs of Westminster Abbey, St Paul's Cathedral, the Chapel Royal, Westminster Cathedral and the Temple Church. In recent years the following singers have been regular members: Roland Tatnell, Timothy Penrose, Adrian Hill, Richard Stevens, and Frederic Hodgson, altos; Harry Barnes, John Dudley, Alfred Hepworth, Keith Abbs, Gordon Pullin and Adrian Goss, tenors; Kenneth Tudor, Roger Cleverdon, Rodney Williams, Howard Thomas and Mark Wildman, basses; with David Robleau and Roger Cleverdon as accompanists.

Throughout its history, famous singers have been members and equally famous composers have written for the Club.

Both in London and the principal provincial towns there were numerous glee clubs during the 18th and 19th centuries, and most of them generously enabled new composers to show their paces by offering prizes for competition. Of these other clubs the Glee Club, founded in 1787 − meeting first in a coffee house and thereafter in various London Taverns − was prominent. George Elvey, who had only just taken up his appointment (at the age of 20!) as organist of St George's, Windsor, hoped that a successful entry in a Glee Competition would be good for his reputation and accordingly submitted a work. About this, Lady Elvey had this to say:[1]

[1] *Reminiscences of Sir George Elvey*, London, 1893. ·

In the spring of 1836 the Glee Club in London offered a ten-guinea prize for the best serious glee, but omitted to state that only members of the Club were allowed to compete. Mr Elvey sent in a composition *O Power Supreme!*, which was examined with the others on the appointed day. When the name of the author was unfolded however, he, not being a member of the Club, was ineligible to receive the money, and the only reward he had was being permitted to print on the title-page of his work that it won the prize competition. A few days afterwards the following lines appeared in the press: –

The funds of the Glee Club being in a condition
To afford a reward for a good composition.
The sons of Apollo in conclave agree
That ten pounds shall be given for the best serious glee.
They resolve that the second-best man shall have five,
The design is proclaimed, and the glees are composed,
Under hieroglyphical emblems enclosed,
Sent in, and performed. The best glee is declared.
The party to hail the composer prepared;
And all hushed in suspense when, the seals being broken,
The disclosure appears a mistake to betoken!
The winner, the moment his name is detected,
Not being a member, of course is rejected.
So that out of the list, which at first numbered three,
The two standing candidates victors must be.
And this comfort they glean from the bottle thus burst,
(On the last day of April instead of the first),
That as no rival glees remain for the purse,
None 'tis plain can be better than theirs and none worse.
The joy of the donors has likewise this zest,
That at once they reward both the worst and the best.
'Tis so in a donkey-race, where success depends more
Upon temper than speed.
To fulfill the old adage, though last, yet not least,
The prizes adjudged to the hindermost beast!

The Hodgson Banner

As a teacher of singing, many of my pupils have gained choral scholarships to Oxford and Cambridge, scholarships to the Schools of Music, and appointments to cathedral choirs. Among them there has been a succession of young singers from the choir of the Chapel Royal, Hampton Court Palace, which under the expertise of Gordon Reynolds provided an excellent training ground. One of my pupils worthy of a special mention was a member of that choir for twenty years. He is Brian Neal, who is blind. He is a fine alto and an excellent musician possessing a phenomenal memory and with the assistance of Braille, repertoire holds no problems. He does not regard his blindness as a disability. He is in demand as a piano tuner, and travels round with admirable courage and assurance. His devoted wife, Sheila, took him to Hampton Court by car from Datchet (fourteen miles) for rehearsals on Fridays, and repeated the journey twice on Sundays with unfailing regularity.

After attending Evensong at St George's, Windsor, one day, he said to me: 'If I had to choose between regaining my sight and singing at St George's, I would gladly choose the latter.' On another occasion he told me he had been to a service at King's College, Cambridge (the best part of 100 miles). I asked him how he got there. 'I hitched lifts there and back', he said. 'I have great faith and I am always helped.'

On my retirement from St George's, he was the instigator of a plan for my pupils to make some tangible token of appreciation to me. The scheme was supported by Gordon Reynolds and his son, Nicholas, and Julian Clarkson, both of St John's College, Cambridge, and Peter and Robert Hayward, both of Magdalen College, Oxford. It was decided that a personal banner should be made, and after some research by another friend, George Brooker, it was left to Nicholas Reynolds to produce an original and striking design, showing an open book with three staves and the alto clef sign, surrounded by the badges of the cathedrals and chapels with which I had been associated. Mrs Valerie Waldron, a well-known professional embroidress, was commissioned to do the work, which took a year to complete. I had been kept completely in the dark until an evening in December 1974, when I gave a recital of solos at Hampton Court. My wife and I had been invited to a choir dinner which was to follow the recital, and my two sons and their wives were also present. I had no inkling that the dinner was actually in my honour, and it came as a tremendous surprise when the magnificent banner was unveiled and presented to me. I was deeply touched.

CHAPTER TWELVE

The Chapels Royal at St James's Palace

After retiring from St George's Chapel I was decorated by the Queen at Buckingham Palace with the Royal Victorian Medal.

I began to sing frequently as a deputy at Westminster Abbey, and also at the Chapel Royal and St Paul's. But I was very soon to find myself singing regularly once again in a famous royal choir, when in 1975 I accepted the offer of appointment as a Gentleman of HM Chapels Royal at St James's Palace, under the direction of Timothy Farrell, the brilliant young organist, whom I had known when he was sub-organist of Westminster Abbey.

My interest in the Chapel Royal goes back to my youth, when the choir had two outstanding altos in J Hatherley Clarke and Charles Hawkins. Hatherley Clarke was undoubtedly my hero, and he was generally considered to be one of the greatest of altos. He had a voice of superb quality and exceptional range, and he was a consummate artist with a commanding presence. He was formerly a lay vicar of Westminster Abbey, and was the founder member of the Gresham Singers, a famous quartet which gave four Royal Command Performances, and once appeared at a gala performance at the Paris Opera. He was celebrated for his singing of the exacting alto solos in Bach's *St John Passion*, which he performed over one hundred times in the choir of St Anne's, Soho, often in the presence of royalty. He died in 1975, at the age of 90.

Charles Hawkins had a voice of a remarkably rich quality, and he sang at the Chapel Royal until he was well in his eighties. Such singers as these represent an era when male altos, among them greatly gifted singers, had no alternative but to languish unrecognised outside the cathedral choir or male-voice quartet. The BBC did not recognise the voice until the inception of the Third Programme, and the revival of baroque music, especially that which was produced in England after the Restoration of the Monarchy. The celebrated Alfred Deller, John Whitworth and one or two others were able to blaze a trail into a new era which provided altos with opportunities and a publicity denied to them for at least 150 years. Dr Harold Watkins Shaw, writing in the *Musical Times* in March 1983, made the point that, 25 years earlier, Deller might have remained in obscurity?

The services at the Chapel Royal are still a model, and are as dignified as could be found anywhere, with music of the highest standard. The ten boys, or Children, in their scarlet and gold State uniforms, together with the six Gentlemen, in their scarlet cassocks, wing collars, and white bow ties, make an impressive sight. In summer, when services are held in the Queen's Chapel, as the choir processes across Marlborough Gate, crowds of tourists flock to watch the colourful spectacle, and there is much clicking and whirring of cameras.

In his *Notes on the Chapels of St James's Palace*, Colin S Scull, late Serjeant of the Vestry of the Chapels Royal, and formerly a Gentleman of the Chapel Royal, has written a fascinating history of this important royal foundation. I acknowledge with gratitude his permission to quote the following extracts:

I *The Establishment and its musicians*

The two chapels in St James's Palace are used for divine service by the Chapel Royal, which in origin and still in principle is not a building but an establishment: a body of priests and singers to serve the spiritual needs of the Sovereign. The later Anglo-Saxon Kings had chaplains who served also as clerks, and from 1068 the Chancellors of England had the chaplains and the Chancery clerks in their charge. At this time, one of the chaplains was Keeper of the Chapel, with four sergeants to assist him; the chapel then included books, plate, vestments, relics and so on, carried in panniers on two pack horses.

Later, a much larger establishment of priests, singers and servants travelled about England with the King, and their earliest permanent 'chapels' were at the Tower of London, Westminster Palace and Eltham Palace. From about 1349, the Chapel Royal (known variously as the Household Chapel or King's Chapel) has had a Dean, and from 1843, when the Royal Free Chapel of the Household was established, there has been a Sub-Dean. 'The Chappell' went to France with Henry V in 1413, and Mass was sung before Agincourt, and in 1520 with Henry VIII to the Field of the Cloth of Gold, where they sang with the French Royal Chapel. Henry VIII maintained chapels at Green-wich, Hampton Court, St James's, Whitehall and other palaces.

The Chapel Royal employed the finest church musicians, who worked mainly at Greenwich under the Tudors and at Whitehall under the Stuarts. In 1702, Queen Anne moved the choral foundation from the Banqueting House at Whitehall (used after the chapel had been burned in 1698) to St James's Palace. In the vestibule of the chapel there, a board can be seen containing the names of Sub-Deans of the Chapel Royal, and another showing those of organists and musicians, selected from a list of 113 names dating from 1444, when the first Master of the Children was appointed. The board includes all the organists (of whom there were often two or more at one time) and other prominent musicians who served in the choir as Children or Gentlemen, or who, like Handel, were specially appointed Composers. The best known organists were Thomas Tallis, William Byrd, Orlando Gibbons, John Blow, Henry Purcell, Maurice Greene and William Boyce. The tradition of a cathedral-type service is maintained by the six Gentlemen and the ten Children, who are educated at the City of London School, and wear their scarlet and gold State coats when at service. The choir sings each year at the Royal Maundy Service in Whitehall on Remembrance Sunday, and on other occasions appointed by the Sovereign.

The Chapel Royal has been called 'the cradle of English church music', for its great musicians of the past set an example in style of composition and performance that was copied by the cathedrals and great churches of the land.

II *The Chapel Royal, St James's Palace*

There was a leper hospital of St James the Less in the fields beyond the village of Charing, probably founded in about 1100. By 1449 it was used as a convent and was granted by Henry VI to Eton College. (Some medieval slip-tiles, found in 1925 under Colour Court and now on the vestibule wall, are possibly from the convent chapel). In 1531, Henry VIII wanted a house for Anne Boleyn, and exchanged some lands with the Provost of Eton for the Convent. He rebuilt it as the Manor of St James, but few parts of the building remain, apart from the gate house and the chapel. The chapel ceiling, probably copied from an Italian renaissance design, with the paintings attributed to

Holbein, commemorates the short-lived marriage of Henry VIII and Anne of Cleves, and is richly decorated with royal heraldry, cyphers and the names of the Cleve family estates. The painting would have been completed after July 1540, when Anne was divorced, as one panel has the arms of Henry impaled with those of Katherine Howard, his fifth wife. The carved and decorated coat-of-arms over the main door is that of Elizabeth I, who used a lion and dragon as supporters. At the end of the Civil War, Charles I was imprisoned in the Palace, and on 30 January 1649 he received the Sacrament of Holy Communion in the chapel before crossing the park to his execution in Whitehall.

The chapel has been used for many royal marriages, and Queen Victoria and Prince Albert were married there in 1840. The wedding of King George V (the Duke of York) and Queen Mary took place in St James's in 1893. King George gave the present organ in 1925 – a large three-manual and pedal organ by Hill, Norman and Beard, modified and revoiced in 1969.

III *The Queen's Chapel at St James's*

This uniquely fine building, designed in the Palladian style by Inigo Jones, was the first post-Reformation church in England, and was built for Roman Catholic worship. Finished in 1627, it was the private chapel of the bride of Charles I, Henrietta Maria of France, who brought French priests and a bishop as her chaplains. The chapel cost £4,027-0-4 to build, and Inigo Jones' plans included the gilding of 28 coffers of the vaulted ceiling. At least two of the painted consecration crosses have survived, and these can be viewed through small doors inserted in the panelling of the West wall. After the Restoration, the chapel was re-furnished for Catherine of Braganza, Queen of Charles II, who installed a community of Portuguese Franciscans. Her coat of arms (the Stuart arms impaled with those of Portugal) appears over the East window and above the fireplace in the royal gallery. Later, the Chapel was used by Mary of Modena, the Italian second wife of James II, and at that time, Samuel Pepys wrote of his visit to 'the Popish chapel at St James's'.

William III permitted the use of the chapel for Reformed worship by Dutch and French-speaking congregations, and later, Queen Anne opened a German Lutheran Royal Chapel in Friary Court. In 1781 the ministers exhanged chapels, and the smaller chapel was destroyed by fire in 1809. The Queen's Chapel was known as the German Chapel after 1781, and the German Lutherans remained there until 1902.

A Danish Lutheran congregation used the chapel until 1936, and they erected a tablet to the memory of Queen Alexandra, herself a Dane. After Queen Mary came to live at Marlborough House, the chapel was completely restored and given to the use of the Chapel Royal in 1938.

The organ in the gallery was built by Snetzler in 1760 for the chapel of Buckingham Palace, and given to the Lutherans in 1830 by William IV. In 1862 a swell manual and pedals were added by Hill, Norman and Beard, who rebuilt the organ in 1938.

IV *A Royal Peculiar*

This term applies to a church which is not subject to a bishop or archbishop, but whose allegiance is directly to the Sovereign. The most famous examples are the Collegiate Church of St Peter in Westminster (Westminster Abbey), and the Queen's Royal Free Chapel of St George within her castle of Windsor. For several hundred years the Chapel Royal has been administered by the Lord Chamberlain's Office, and maintained by the Privy Purse. The Dean of Her Majesty's Chapels Royal has in his charge the three surviving chapels at St James's Palace, Hampton Court Palace, and HM Tower of London.

Since 1603 the post has been filled by a bishop, and since 1748 by the Bishop of London. He is assisted by a resident Sub-Dean and three Priests in Ordinary to conduct the services. The 36 Chaplains to the Queen, under the Clerk of the Closet (a bishop who is the Sovereign's spiritual adviser), supply the preachers during the year. The Royal Almonry is also part of the ecclesiastical household: headed by the Lord High Almoner (a bishop), it dispenses the Queen's charitable gifts, especially the Royal Maundy.

The Chapels of Hampton Court Palace and HM Tower of London each have a resident Chaplain and fully choral services. The Queen's Chapel of the Savoy is not a Chapel Royal, but belongs to the Queen in right of her Duchy of Lancaster; it is the chapel of the Royal Victorian Order. There is a private Royal Chapel of All Saints in Windsor Great Park (with a resident chaplain), and Private Chapels in Windsor Castle and Buckingham Palace, served by Domestic Chaplains.

The Chapel Royal of today, with its two chapels in St James's Palace, is the inheritor of a thousand years of history, and those who serve in this establishment strive to safeguard the tradition of worship and to maintain the uniquely high standard inherited from their illustrious predecessors over many centuries.[1]

V *Royal Maundy Services*

There are two occasions in the year when a wider public is made aware of the existence of the choir of the Chapel Royal. One is a ceremony of the Sunday in November which serves to remind us of the great European wars (in particular of this century). The other is the Royal Maundy Service, which in recent years has helped to show us the beauty of some of our most famous buildings and the enhancement of such beauty by that of the music of the Cathedral traditions. The particular service is held on Maundy Thursday (hence its name) and it dates from the 12th century. Its features are the carrying of traditional nosegays and the distribution by the Monarch of Maundy Money to selected recipients.

The old Chapel Royal in Whitehall was the scene in former times for many of these services, and from 1892 to 1952 they were held in Westminster Abbey. But during the reign of Elizabeth II it has become the custom to hold them in other places:

1953 St Paul's	1974 Salisbury	1986 Chichester
1955 Southwark	1975 Peterborough	1987 Ely
1957 St Albans	1976 Hereford	1988 Lichfield
1959 Windsor	1978 Carlisle	1989 Birmingham
1961 Rochester	1979 Winchester	1990 Newcastle
1963 Chelmsford	1980 Worcester	1991 Westminster Abbey
1965 Canterbury	1982 St David's	1992 Chester
1967 Durham	1983 Exeter	1993 Wells
1969 Selby	1984 Southwell	1994 Truro
1971 Tewkesbury	1985 Ripon	1995 Coventry
1972 York		

[1] For a comprehensive history of the Chapel Royal, see *The Chapel Royal Ancient and Modern*, by David Baldwin (Duckworth, 1990).

The Chapel Royal choir always takes part wherever the service is held, and joins forces with the resident choir. The scarlet and gold State uniforms of the Children of the Chapel Royal add a touch of brilliance to the scene. Traditionally they lead the procession.

My first experience of singing at a Maundy Service was as a lay clerk of St George's Chapel, Windsor, in 1959, where it was held for the first time in the existing chapel. I well remember how Harry Gabb, the Chapel Royal organist, directed the two choirs with his usual persuasion and charm, and Sir William Harris provided some fine organ accompaniments. One of my alto colleagues on that occasion was Charles Hawkins, and I was intrigued with his admirable tone. Being then in his late seventies he showed the benefits of a wonderful technique.

It was not until 1976 that I sang at another Maundy Service, this time as a Gentleman of the Chapel Royal. The service was held at Hereford as part of the celebrations commemorating the founding of the See 1300 years ago. The two choirs responded excellently under the conductorship of Roy Massey, the Hereford organist, who was ably supported by his assistant, Robert Green. A special feature was the superb organ accompaniment of Handel's *Zadok the Priest* by Timothy Farrell, the Chapel Royal organist. The pleasure of my visit to Hereford was heightened by the warmth of hospitality extended to me by my alto friend, Alan Stewart, senior lay clerk and his wife, Olga.

In 1977, Jubilee Year, the service was held appropriately in Westminster Abbey, and here we were on familiar ground. The direction of the music under Douglas Guest, with Stephen Cleobury at the organ, guaranteed that magnificent singing and organ playing always associated with the Abbey.

Carlisle was the scene for the 1978 ceremony. The occasion was a particularly great one for the city, as the Queen had not visited it for twenty years, and she was greeted enthusiastically by tremendous crowds. The music at the service was very fine under Andrew Sievewright, the Cathedral organist, who conducted the choirs, with excellent organ accompaniments by his assistant, Hugh Davies.

The Gentlemen of the Chapel Royal were accommodated comfortably at the Castle Hotel, where an entry in my diary recalls the following incident:

We first had lunch at the hotel, where we were invited to try the local delicacy known as Cumberland Sausage. We were astonished and amused when it arrived, as it was nearly ten inches long and curled round almost the whole of the plate! But its rather indecent looks belied its excellent taste, and it provided a memorable example of that northern hospitality which is prepared to go to any lengths.

1979 provided an outstanding occasion at Winchester, where the cathedral was celebrating its 900th anniversary. Here the music was of a superlatively high standard under Martin Neary (now organist of Westminster Abbey), who was himself one of the Children of the Chapel Royal and sang at the Coronation in 1953, and his excellent assistant James Lancelot (now organist or Durham Cathedral). A notable feature was the splendid singing by Winchester boys of Mendelssohn's *I waited for the Lord.*

Among the anthems sung at Maundy Services, according to tradition, the following are included: *Lord, for Thy tender mercy's sake* (Anon, 16th century), *Wash me throughly* (Wesley), and *Zadok the Priest* (Handel). In 1980 the service was held at Worcester Cathedral. The Chapel Royal choir travelled to Worcester by coach, and the Gentlemen were accommodated at the Giffard Hotel in the H gh Street, which commands fine views of the Cathedral. The Children of the Chapel were staying in College Green, where they soon made friends with a black cat which they had the wit to name 'Zadok', as appropriate to an occasion when Handel's *Zadok the Priest* was to be sung. The opening words are: 'Zadok, the Priest, and Nathan the prophet, anointed Solomon King'. It was fortuitous that another cat should appear at our hotel, and although he greeted me with a very high-pitched miaow, I accepted the remarkable luxuriance of his 'Handel-bar (!) whiskers as his badge of masculinity, and I dubbed him 'Nathan'. But I looked in vain for a 'Solomon'!

On the Wednesday afternoon we attended a procession rehearsal, which was followed by a rehearsal of the combined choirs of the Cathedral and the Chapel Royal. In the evening the gentlemen much appreciated being entertained to a sumptuous dinner by the Worcester lay clerks.

Maundy Thursday was a delightful sunny day, and Worcester looked at its best, with streets decorated gaily to welcome the Queen.

The Royal Maundy Procession is always a superb spectacle, which is reflected in the expressions of wonder and pleasurable anticipation on the face of the recipients. It was a memorable sight to look down the Cathedral, with its huge congregation, and the whole setting enhanced by a glorious blaze of light from the West Window.

The singing of the combined choirs, conducted by Dr Donald Hunt, the Cathedral organist, and Richard Popplewell, the Chapel Royal organist, was remarkably fine. The Cathedral assistant organist, Paul Trepte (now organist of Ely Cathedral), provided excellent organ accompaniments.

VI *The Silver Jubilee*

Having taken part in so many royal occasions, it was particularly gratifying to me to sing with the Chapel Royal choir in the Thanksgiving Service held in St Paul's Cathedral on 7th June, 1977, to mark the Queen's Silver Jubilee. I was one of the few to have sung at the Queen's Coronation and also at her Jubilee. On 6th June a rehearsal was held for men's voices only (the boys had rehearsed in the morning). There were eighteen Vicars Choral of St Paul's, and six Gentlemen of the Chapel Royal. The rehearsal took place in the Song School in the Crypt, and was conducted by Christopher Dearnley, organist, and Barry Rose, sub-organist, and all went extremely well in a relaxed atmosphere. We had a break for tea in the BBC canteen, which had been installed in the Crypt for the occasion. A full rehearsal followed in the Cathedral, with the Trumpeters from Kneller Hall, and what a superb sound it all made, enhanced by the famous echo. The Chapel Royal choir was seated Decani and Cantoris on small platforms at the end of the choir stalls.

Jubilee day was cold, windy and showery, and reminiscent of the weather on Coronation Day. I went off to Windsor Riverside Station at 6.30 am in my pinstripe suit, trilby hat (plus 'classical curve'), and umbrella. Later, one of my colleagues said: 'You look a proper city gent.' (But how I rejoiced when I saw one of the young Vicars Choral of St Paul's resplendent in full grey morning dress!) In my bag I had my hood, medals, music, extra glasses, food, throat pastilles, and just in case, indigestion tablets, as throat pastilles after food invite repercussions. Even at that early hour there was a queue for tickets, and Waterloo Station was crowded when I arrived. We had been advised to avoid the processional route, and I walked from Piccadilly Circus to St James's Palace. I went into the Mall for a moment and as I mingled with the dense crowds of many nationalities and listened to the excited chatter, believe it or not, there just had to be the unmistakeable and so familiar sound of that Sheffield voice which never fails to predominate on any occasion anywhere at any time. Above all the cosmopolitan hubbub there rose – 'We'll be alreight 'ere lass, tha knows, and when we've had summat t'eat, we'll get nearer t'front'. That voice bridged a gap of years and I went on my way feeling no stranger.

The choir robed and then boarded a coach to take us to St Paul's. The waiting crowds spotted the scarlet and gold uniforms of the Children, and the red cassocks and white bows of the Gentlemen through the coach window, and we received continuous cheers and flag-waving all the way to St Paul's. Duty passes had to be shown to enter the Cathedral.

Following a short rehearsal, the two choirs lined up in the Dean's Aisle for the Ecclesiastical Procession, and the atmosphere was one of excitement as we moved to the east side of the Dome to our place in the choir. As I stepped on to a small platform, I tripped over a piece of carpet which had come unstuck, but I soon recovered as if nothing had happened. It is curious how these small incidents can recall similar ones in the past, and there flashed through my mind that first 'trip' as a tiny choirboy not yet six years old stumbling up the chancel steps at St Simon's, Sheffield (a 'good omen', my father had said!).

The Ecclesiastical Procession was a lengthy one, and was led by a verger and the two choirs, followed by the Commissary, the Chapter Clerk and minor canons. The Salvation Army and the Free Churches were represented, and then came the Roman Catholic Archbishop of Westminster, the Moderator of the General Assembly of the Church of Scotland, and the Prebendaries and Archdeacons. There were Suffragan Bishops, the Serjeant of the Vestry of HM Chapels Royal, the Deans of Westminster and Windsor, and the Clerk of the Closet, the Lord High Almoner, the Archbishops of Wales and Armagh, and the Archbishop of York. The Archbishop of Canterbury, the Bishop of London, and the Dean and Chapter were in the Queen's Procession.

It was gratifying to see bodies other than the Church of England well represented; even so the service was afterwards criticised for being too exclusively Anglican in form.

As I looked down the great floodlit Cathedral, with its congregation of 2700, it was a memorable spectacle. Above all there was an astonishing blaze of colour – from women's hats at the one end of the scale to the glitter of spurs and swords, and the splendour of uniforms, at the other. The Gentlemen-At-Arms in their scarlet coats and plumed helmets provided a specially magical touch of colour. There was an air of expectancy over the whole building, which provided the perfect setting for an occasion which had captured a worldwide interest. There were 500 million television viewers. State Trumpeters of the Household Cavalry heralded the Queen's entry at the West Door, and the procession moved up the nave to the hymn: *All people that on earth do dwell* ('Old Hundreth tune' to the Coronation arrangement by Vaughan Williams), in which the Trumpeters of the Royal Military School at Kneller Hall came into their own. Psalm 121, *I will lift up mine eyes*, was sung to a chant by Barry Rose, sub-organist (later choirmaster of St Paul's and now organist of St Alban's Cathedral). The first lesson was followed by Parry's magnificent anthem, *I was glad* (written for the Coronation in 1902), and here the trumpeters added to the accompaniment with thrilling effect. The traditional 'Vivats' were included, as at Coronations. There were further prayers and two hymns – *O God of Bethel* and *Immortal, invisible* – before the short address given by the Archbishop of Canterbury, Dr Coggan, who likened the monarchy to a house built on firm foundations: 'It is something at the heart of our national life of incalculable value – a spirit of devotion to duty, and of service to others which has found its focus in a family and a person.' Then came the hymn *Praise my soul* and a short anthem composed for the occasion by Christopher Dearnley, organist of St Paul's: *Let Thy hand be strengthened*. More prayers and then Vaughan Williams' stirring *Te Deum* in G rang out triumphantly.

After the blessing by the Archbishop of Canterbury, the service concluded with the National Anthem, arranged by Gordon Jacob. We had a last look at the memorable scene as we processed out and we returned to the Chapel Royal by Coach. As we disrobed, we all agreed it had been a wonderful occasion in which it was a privilege to have taken part.

Members of the Chapel Royal choir who took part were: Children– Neil Thomas, Mark Thomas, Giles Stockton, Gavin Kibble, Robert Sawdy, Colin Campbell, Bruce Trathen, Richard Cave, John Coutts,

Michael Hughes; Gentlemen- Peter Goldspink (alto), Frederic Hodgson (alto), Norman Cooper (tenor), Richard Lewis (tenor), Richard Edwards (bass), Graham Trew (bass).

The Gentlemen and Children afterwards received the Queen's Silver Jubilee Medal.

VII *The baptism of Peter Mark Andrew Phillips*

A royal domestic occasion which called for a musical presence was the baptism of Princess Anne's son, Peter Mark Andrew Phillips, at Buckingham Palace on 22nd December 1977. After a short rehearsal at the Chapel Royal we put on our cassocks and then went by coach to the Palace, where we completed robing. The service took place in the music room, an elegant setting with gold, white and blue the dominant colours. The choir was placed by a window, and Timothy Farrell accompanied us on a Broadwood grand. The then Archbishop of Canterbury, Donald Coggan, conducted the service and baptised the child in the Lily Font, customarily used for Royal Baptisms, and made in 1840 for the children of Queen Victoria to be baptised. Canon James Mansel, Sub-Dean of the Chapels Royal and Domestic Chaplain to the Queen, assisted the Archbishop. The Order of Service – the Alternative Services Second Series – was used for the first time for a royal baptism.

As an introit we sang Weelkes's *Let Thy merciful ears*, and later Walford Davies's *A babe lies in the cradle* (Spiritual Songs, No 1). From this the singing of the opening solo by Neil Thomas, Head Child of the Chapel Royal, lingers in the memory.

In latter years it has been my pleasure to sing frequently in the choir of the Chapel Royal at Hampton Court Palace.

* * *

I shall hope to go on singing as long as I am spared. My birthday is on the 22nd day of the month, and Psalm 108, set for that day, could not be more appropriate: 'O God, my heart is ready, my heart is ready, I will sing and give praise with the best member that I have.'

On the future of church music, Archbishop Lang's words remain true: 'The great tradition of English Church Music is a sacred trust, and the offering of music is a true part of worship. Whatever changes there may be at hand in the Church, as well as in the State, it is to be hoped that there will be no restraint of that river of noble music consecrated by the spirit of worship, which has for centuries made glad the City of God.'

Overleaf: Stone's setting of the Lord's Prayer, edited and transcribed by CF Simkins.

THE LORD'S PRAIER.

Robt. Stone. (Stones).
(1516--1613.)

(S.) Our Father, which art in heaven, Hallow-ed be Thy Name.

(A) Our Father, which art in heaven, Hallow-ed be Thy Name.

(T) Our Father, which art in heaven, Hallow-ed be Thy Name.

(B) Our Father, which art in heaven, Hallow-ed be Thy Name.

Thy king-dom come, Thy will be done in earth as it is in heaven.

Thy king-dom come, Thy will be done in earth as it is in heaven.

Thy kingdom come, Thy will be done in earth, as it is in heaven.

Thy kingdom come, Thy will be done in earth, as it is in heaven.

* This Meane part is for men. (Day).

C.F.S.1.

[115]

INDEX